Get Your Startup Story Straight

"I raised $4 million for my startup in July by reading this book, and you can, too. I know it was the book because I had been out fundraising for six months with little luck when David Riemer sent me *Get Your Startup Story Straight*. Although, I had my pitch down pat and really was kind of loving it, I opened David's book in case there were any insights I might apply. By the time I'd motored all the way to the end, I had mentally torn up my tried and true (and failing) pitch and crystallized a fresh plan of attack for my meeting the next day. I chucked the stats and graphs and marketingspeak. Instead, I followed Dr. Riemer's prescription: I told a story. No one knows your startup's story better than you do. And as you're about to discover, no one knows how to help you tell it better than David Riemer."

—Jon Klein, former president, CNN US;
cofounder, Hang Media

"Entrepreneurs and innovators have big dreams of changing the world with a grand vision. But that's not enough. The key to making a big impact is to articulate the vision to be compelling and exciting, to wow a group of super talented people, partners, and investors to believe and support the cause. The best way to do so is by transforming an abstract vision into a vivid story, and this is exactly what David's inspiring book will help you do."

—Brad Bao, co-founder and chairman of Lime, named in Time Magazine's "100 Most Infl

D1410501

"Having worked with hundreds of early startup founders, they all could have benefited from reading this and using the tools and frameworks from this book. Cannot recommend this book enough."

—Marvin Liao, partner at GameGroove Capital and former partner at 500 Startups

"As a VC focused on investing at the inception-stage, I've heard tens of thousands of pitches. And the most common feedback we share is to get the story straight! David's *Get Your Startup Story Straight* will not only improve your chances of winning investor capital, but will also help you narrow your focus at a most critical time of company formation. For those further along in their entrepreneurial journey, *Get Your Startup Story Straight* is packed with easy-to-implement strategies to get you back on course. A must read for any entrepreneur!"

—Michael Berolzheimer, founder and managing partner, Bee Partners

"I am so glad David wrote this book so I did not have to. Building successful startups is about so much more than novel technologies—it is about solving big problems for customers woven into a beautiful story. David is the master of teaching storytelling by telling stories."

—Sonja Hoel Perkins, founder of The Perkins Fund, Broadway Angels, and Project Glimmer; former partner, Menlo Ventures

"My advice to innovators: Tell 'em you're painting a picture. Then tell 'em the story that paints the picture. And if you want to know how to do that, you need to read this book. It's David Riemer in action."

—Rich Lyons, chief innovation officer, UC Berkeley; former dean, Berkeley-Haas School of Business

"Behind every company and every product there is a story. These stories are what ultimately define your company and they are the ones that connect your users with your product. David is a master of uncovering and telling these stories. I had the privilege of working with David to tell the first stories of both Databricks and Anyscale, stories which were instrumental in putting these companies on the map. If you are an entrepreneur or want to become one, this is a must-read book!"

—Ion Stoica, executive chairman, Databricks; executive chairman and president, Anyscale

GET YOUR STARTUP STORY STRAIGHT

The Definitive Storytelling Framework
for Innovators and Entrepreneurs

DAVID RIEMER

RIVER GROVE
BOOKS

Published by River Grove Books
Austin, TX
www.rivergrovebooks.com

Distributed by River Grove Books

Design and composition by Greenleaf Book Group
Cover design by Greenleaf Book Group
For permission to reproduce copyrighted material, grateful acknowledgment is made to the following:
ALEXANDER HAMILTON (from the Broadway musical "Hamilton")
Words and Music by LIN-MANUEL MIRANDA
© 2015 5000 BROADWAY MUSIC (ASCAP)
All Rights Administered by WC MUSIC CORP.
All Rights Reserved
Used by Permission of ALFRED MUSIC

Photo of Databricks website. Copyright © 2014 by Databricks.
All rights reserved. Used by permission.

Publisher's Cataloging-in-Publication data is available.

Paperback ISBN: 978-1-63299-469-1

Hardcover ISBN: 978-1-63299-473-8

eBook ISBN: 978-1-63299-472-1

First Edition

To the idea people:
To the creative thinkers who have the big ideas.
To the visionaries who have strong enough
convictions to develop them.
To the courageous ones willing to take on
every obstacle to make it all happen.

>>>⟶

Every successful
innovation has a story.

CONTENTS

Foreword

I raised $4 million for my startup in July by reading this book, and you can too. I know it was the book because I had been out fundraising for six months with little luck when David Riemer happened to send me the galleys for *Get Your Startup Story Straight*. He had no idea I was in the middle of raising a round; he was just seeking input from entrepreneurs. Besides being a close friend since college, David had headed up marketing at a startup I'd founded twenty years ago, before leaving to do the same for Yahoo!.

The book arrived one day before my call with a Silicon Valley VC—an experienced investor who had been a seed funder in unicorns like Uber and Salesforce. A major leaguer who could put my company on the map. Although I had my pitch down pat and really was kind of loving it, I opened David's book in case there were any insights I might apply.

To be honest, I doubted there would be. I mean, I've been launching startups for over thirty years and have raised more than $100 million from stellar VCs and acquirers, including Ron Conway's Silicon Valley Angels, Warburg Pincus, Apple, Discovery, and Intel. What's more, I've been a professional storyteller for five decades, as a news and documentary producer for CBS and a screenwriter for studios including Disney, Paramount, and MGM. As a startup CEO I might need advice on the intricacies of managing a customer acquisition funnel or how to code an unstructured machine-learning brain. But the one thing I sure didn't need advice about was telling the story of my startup.

Boy was I wrong. That was clear before I'd even gotten through chapter one. And by the time I'd motored all the way to the end, I had mentally torn up my tried-and-true (and failing) pitch and crystallized a fresh plan of attack for my meeting the next day. I chucked the stats and graphs and marketingspeak. Instead, I followed Dr. Riemer's prescription: I told a story.

"It's a love story," I began, on the next day's Zoom call. Right off the bat that was a catchier way to describe the two-sided market we had recognized than using the term "two-sided market." We connect professional athletes looking to monetize their downtime with sports fans eager for face time with their heroes. Like "When Harry Met Sally," each provides something the other desperately needs. That's what I said—because David said to say that. I had never thought of my company that way before, but as I spoke, it made perfect sense. Whether I got this guy's money or not, I was going to think differently about my company, who it was serving, and how I could over-deliver to them.

My tale ended with the line "All we need is $4 million to make this love story come true." Upon which the investor replied, "I can get you $4 million in two weeks." And then he set about doing it. It was that simple and straightforward. In my many years of raising startup capital, nothing like that had ever happened. And it only happened because I read this book.

In retrospect, it makes perfect sense that David would be the one to unearth the company narrative caked beneath my layers of jargon. He's a naturally gifted raconteur who wrote musical comedies in college and was chosen by our fellow students to deliver the commencement address. But crucially, those mad right-brain skills are complemented by a left-brain knack for clear-headed analysis. He's the most creative MBA you'll ever meet. David instinctively understands that all great stories begin with a blueprint. When David was a hot-shot advertising executive at J. Walter Thompson, I would toss him grabby slogans he could use for his Sprint or IBM accounts. And he would patiently explain that the catchphrases come last—first comes a deep understanding of the customer those companies are trying to reach, what they need, and how the product meets that need. Figure that out, and the words will flow.

Same with a startup.

No one knows your startup's story better than you do. And as you're about to discover, no one knows how to help you tell it better than David Riemer.

—Jon Klein
Cofounder at HANG Media
Former President, CNN/US

Preface

I wrote my first story in third grade. I called it "How the Koala Bear Got His Pouch." It was awful. My story was missing most of the elements that make a good narrative, but I was clearly compelled to *tell* stories.

As a teenager, I wrote for newspapers and a magazine. By the time I got to college, I was writing plays. I spoke at my graduation and found a way to work a story into the speech. For the speech, I invented a narrative about a homeless person named Flo.

I have a great story about that story.

I gave that speech in the First Unitarian Church of Providence, where Brown University holds its graduations. It's a daunting place to give an address. I was standing before a thousand classmates in the old pews of a place of worship built in the eighteenth century.

Right before going on, I saw my uncle, who advised me, "Don't make a schmuck of yourself." It was a fair warning. One of my best friends, Jon Klein, who is smarter and much funnier than I, went before me. No pressure. I gave my talk and somehow survived. I saw my uncle on the college green shortly thereafter. "You peaked at twenty-two," he dryly told me. I graduated, packed up my room, and started my career. I thought the speech was behind me.

Four years later, I ended my first year of graduate school in New York City, and I was moving apartments. Normally, packing is a tedious chore, but this time I was doing it with a cute classmate named Carla, which made it a bit more fun. While cleaning out an old shoebox, I found a cassette tape. I held it up and proudly said, "This is a recording of my college graduation speech. Want to hear it?" I'm sure she was thinking, *Really? Do I have to listen to this?* But she said, "Sure!" I put the tape in the cassette deck, pressed play, and after a few moments she said, "Stop the tape." I said, "Why?" She said, "Just stop it."

Carla, who I'd known only a few months, then told me what the rest of the speech was about.

It turns out that Carla's favorite cousin was a college class-mate of mine and a good friend of my roommate, and Carla had attended my graduation years before we met. And she remembered my speech. Why? Because I told a story:

> I was sitting on the college green in my final days as
> a student when a paper I was writing was whisked
> away in a gust of wind down College Hill. I raced

after the pages all the way downtown, where I encountered a homeless person named Flo. It was a wake-up call. Flo had lived a hard life and told me what the world was *really* like.

I created the story to make a point about life in our ivory tower being over. It was time to engage with people like Flo. It was time to face the real world.

It turned out Carla didn't have special powers, but I had used a special power without realizing it: storytelling. My story was vivid enough to be memorable. Or maybe it was destiny? Shortly after that, we started dating. Thirty-three years ago, we got married and now have two wonderful adult children. And I'm still telling stories.

From Loving Stories to Making a Living with Stories

I've weaved storytelling throughout my career, which has spanned nonprofits, the ad biz, the tech-marketing world, higher ed, and the theater business. Living in the Bay Area for most of my adult life, I've been working in and around innovators. It eventually dawned on me that a strong story was always at the heart of great innovation. While teaching at Berkeley-Haas School of Business, I often watched students in applied innovation programs struggle when they didn't have a clear narrative in mind. Their ideas weren't terribly fresh, and they couldn't communicate the concepts clearly.

I saw the same thing working with many entrepreneurs at several Bay Area accelerators. But once these innovators started thinking through and developing the story, everything fell into place—the quality of the ideas and the ease of talking about them.

When I started to dig deeper, I learned that there's actual brain science behind why stories are so useful and compelling. Stories are in our DNA. Stories are powerful. In Lisa Cron's great book *Wired for Story* she argues that story is what makes us human. She says, "Recent breakthroughs in neuroscience reveal that our brain is hardwired to respond to story; the pleasure we derive from a tale well told is nature's way of seducing us into paying attention to it. Story, as it turns out, was crucial to our evolution—more so than opposable thumbs. Opposable thumbs let us hang on; story told us what to hang on to."[1] We'll explore more about this in Act 2 of the book.

Stories are immensely helpful in focusing people who are determined to create something new. Jack Dorsey, the founder of Twitter and Square, commented about the power of story: "One of the biggest things that has helped me is learning how to become a better storyteller and the power of a story. If you want to build a product—and you want to build a product that's relevant to folks—you need to put yourself in their shoes and need to write a story from their side . . . so we write user narratives of (for example) this user, who's in the middle of Chicago and this is the experience they're going to have and it reads like a play."[2]

---

1   Lisa Cron, *Wired for Story* (Clarkson Potter/Ten Speed, 2012), Introduction.

2   Jack Dorsey, "The Power of Curiosity and Inspiration," Stanford University Entrepreneurial Thought Leaders Seminar (lecture viewable on YouTube), February 9, 2011.

This exploration inspired me to develop the seminar Storytelling for Innovation in my role as executive-in-residence at Berkeley-Haas. It uses a classic narrative framework as a backdrop to help people nurture and develop innovative ideas. It forces innovators to pursue a deep understanding of the customer, who is the main character in their story.

Since then, I've further developed this thinking in my work with hundreds of entrepreneurs. I've begun to share these ideas with audiences in places as far-flung as Hyderabad, Vancouver, and Istanbul. Everyone understands stories—that's why we're here.

Welcome to *Get Your Startup Story Straight*.

Introduction

Today, anyone can become an innovator—on your own or within an organization. You can and often need to innovate quickly. It used to take an overwhelming amount of time and capital to create or operationalize a new product or service. Now it can happen overnight.

When the COVID-19 pandemic hit, most businesses had to innovate in a flash. This was especially true in the healthcare sector, where large institutions had to deploy mobile health applications, ramp up telehealth offerings, provide massive testing operations, modify ICUs, and create entirely new systems for the patient-intake process. Every aspect required reinvention.

I recently met Dr. Panna Lossy, who was working at an early COVID testing site in northern California when she realized the process was fundamentally flawed. Dr. Lossy met an older woman with COVID symptoms who was in a car full of family members. The doctor learned that one of the woman's grown children back at home was undergoing chemotherapy. To make matters worse, the family's next stop was Costco, where she'd be shoulder to shoulder with dozens of people! The person in the car wouldn't get her test back for days, but she was likely infected. She was about to expose others to the virus, including vulnerable family members. The doctor had no tools to guide this patient into self-isolation so she wouldn't be a danger to others. Dr. Lossy was horrified, and she set out to fix the problem. She created an organization called IsoCare to help COVID patients and suspected patients learn how to safely isolate themselves, their family members, and their communities.

The year 2020 reminded us just how quickly we need to adjust and change how we do things. Today, with the ability to communicate from anywhere and easily tap into outsourced services, it is much easier than ever before to design, manufacture, market, and ship a new product or launch a new service. Innovators are ubiquitous nowadays, and for this community storytelling is—in pandemic parlance—an essential service.

Get Your Startup Story Straight is for entrepreneurs and intrapreneurs looking to solve problems or create something new. You could be solving a business problem, developing a new product or service, or creating a new way for your organization to conduct business. It's a how-to book that walks you through the steps of building and telling a story. It helps structure your thinking and forces you to deeply understand your customers and pinpoint how your innovation will improve their lives.

In the book, I will talk about the essential elements that compose a good story. I'll share examples of innovators who were particularly good at understanding—and sharpening—their story (and maybe some who weren't). The cases will include businesses large and small, as well as institutions and nonprofit organizations. One of these examples is a cloud-data platform company called Databricks. I started working on the Databricks story with the UC Berkeley professor and the two Berkeley PhDs who cofounded the company just seven years ago. Together, we created a narrative about the protagonist in their story—a data scientist who struggled to fulfill the promise of discovering game-changing business insights from all the user information the company was collecting. The Databricks platform cleared many of the hurdles their customers faced and delivered on its promise of making it easier for these specialists to find answers in the data. Today, thanks to extraordinary technology, smart execution, and a little help from a compelling story, Databricks has over five thousand customers, has $275M in revenue, and is valued at $38B. According to Forbes, they're the eighth-largest startup in the world. You'll hear more about this narrative later in the book.

In Act 1 of *Startup Story*, I share how you can dramatically improve your product and business by seeing the world through the lens of a strong narrative. You will be better equipped to grasp the relationship between your customer and your service, enabling you to better focus your product development efforts. In Act 2, I demonstrate how storytelling techniques enable you to talk clearly about your innovation and inspire others to become wild fans of it—be they customers, investors, or employees. In Act 3, I share a few common innovation story archetypes that might resonate with your own innovation story. If one of these archetypes feels familiar to your story, you can use it to jump-start your narrative.

If you are reading this book to enhance your pitches, you'll be glad that you did, but you should *also* use this book to learn how to use story to guide your product strategy and shape your company. After all, you can't *tell* a great story unless you *have* a great story to tell. You need to be sure that you have all the necessary elements of a compelling product story in place before you can develop exciting ways to tell it. *Get Your Startup Story Straight* helps you build that story and make it magical.

>>>→

Act 1

How to Build a Great Story

1

Stories Matter

"This is supposed to be the best day of my life," Matt Cooper told me. "It's the birth of my son . . . I'm standing there in the delivery room . . . then suddenly, the physicians are calling for life-saving drugs." Matt's voice caught as he recollected the emotions roiling through him in that moment. He paused and then recalled wondering, "Oh, my God, is this going to be the worst day of my life?"

Matt started telling me this story at a Berkeley-Haas alumni event where I gave a talk on storytelling. He wanted to affirm what I was saying: Stories matter.

Matt Cooper is a PhD in toxicology and a biotech entrepreneur who needed to raise money for his new company, Carmenta Bioscience. Carmenta sought a better way to detect preeclampsia, a potentially deadly complication of pregnancy. Matt thought the best way to hone his pitch would be first to find venture capitalists who didn't invest in this type of biotech. He'd work out the kinks in his presentation on this friendly audience, refine his story, then target venture people who were *better* prospects for an actual investment.

Matt arranged a meeting with a woman in a firm that had never invested in a company like Carmenta. She was the perfect person to provide feedback. The pitch plodded along until finally she asked him, "Why are you doing this?" *What do you mean?* Matt wondered. She repeated, "Why are you doing *this?* Why did you choose *this* particular area of science?" Matt could hardly get a word out before tearing up. Through his tears, he told her the story that he shared with me that evening.

He described how his wife, Amy, nearly died of a misdiagnosis of preeclampsia during the birth of his son Zach. As they brought the life-saving drugs into the delivery room to save Amy, Matt made the statement that made me choke up when I heard it: "The best day of my life might become the worst." They were having a baby in a top Boston hospital, and the ob-gyn was a teacher at Harvard—and even *she* missed the diagnosis. Amy survived and so did Zach, but the experience was life changing for Matt. As a biotech professional and entrepreneur, he knew the misdiagnosis was a problem that needed solving.

Matt was embarrassed that he had cried in a professional setting. He only realized later that he had employed some of the most powerful storytelling tools available to an innovator trying to inspire others about his idea. He made himself vulnerable by telling a *personal* story about one of the most critical moments in his life. He tapped into emotion by sharing this pivotal part of the story, which made him choke up. He brought the customer into the room by explaining the crisis that he and his wife faced. He romanced the problem by noting that even a top ob-gyn couldn't recognize this condition in advance. In short, he moved his audience in a way he never expected or even hoped.

Matt's story so compelled the VC that her company made its first investment *ever* in this sector. Matt was off and running with his fundraising. He never intended to tell this personal story—and he certainly couldn't imagine that he would ever cry in a business meeting—but that was before he understood the power of a riveting story. Now Matt knows that telling the right story is essential if you want your new idea to see the light of day.

Hopefully, you see some of yourself in Matt. You see a person who is committed to making things better, who is determined to solve problems. Like Matt, you don't accept the status quo. You don't do something because that's the way it's always been done. You are one of those people who toils like crazy and fights the battles necessary to create something new. And like Matt, you want to be successful.

However, you know how hard it is—most new ideas never make it—and you want to develop every tool in your arsenal to become the exception to the rule. Most people don't appreciate the role a good story plays in their ability to make innovation happen. But Matt Cooper's story illustrates just how powerful one can be.

Most successful entrepreneurs are driven by the belief that there's a better way. They envision a future world with their product in it that's better than the current world without it. The best entrepreneurs know exactly what problem they're trying to solve and for whom they are solving it. Once they know that, once they really know their audience, they keep the customer top of mind. They constantly consider their frustrations, challenges, preferences, and whims.

These creators are effectively writing a story, and this customer—whose life they're trying to improve—is the protagonist in that story. By comparison, many aspiring innovators with brilliant ideas struggle—and often fail—when they don't know who their customer is or don't pinpoint a very specific place to start.

Matt's experience with this venture capitalist demonstrates the power of storytelling to help persuade an audience. But to be successful as an entrepreneur, Matt needed more than proof of his passion for solving this problem. He also needed a great product story that demonstrated a deep understanding of his customer, a clear sense of the problem he was going to solve, and a solution that did so better than the existing alternatives. Were there certain types of women more prone to suffering the condition of preeclampsia? What is it like trying to manage one's health during pregnancy, and how does that inform potential steps toward early detection? How do doctors and patients currently monitor the health of pregnant women to identify this condition? The answers to these and other questions would inform Matt's product narrative.

Rarely does a great product story simply manifest itself. Rather, the story typically emerges over time based on ongoing discovery. An innovator like Matt must tirelessly develop hypotheses and continually refine his story based on user feedback to make sure he is getting the story straight. The best place to start to build a great product story is to understand narrative structure.

Narrative Structure

During the COVID-19 pandemic, our family was often looking for fun activities. Completing the Disney-Pixar bracket was high on the list. Using the popular NCAA basketball tournament bracket format, fans of Disney and Pixar films created various brackets pitting dozens of Disney and Pixar movies against each other. You must choose between a series of pairs of Disney and Pixar films until you've arrived at your all-time favorite. You may agonize over some of the choices (*The Incredibles* or *Wall-E*?!). It's hard; some of the world's most successful storytellers created these films.

Pixar typically takes up to five years making a film and at least four of those just working out the story. They understand the number-one principle of storytelling: You can't *tell* a good story if you don't *have* a good story to tell. You must build a strong narrative structure first.

Robert McKee, Hollywood's most famous screenwriting guru, describes story structure this way: "Story is rooted in causal logic. . . . A story begins when something throws life out of balance. . . . There are forces in opposition to you that will resist your efforts. . . . Eventually, you will be able to restore balance."[3]

Aaron Sorkin, the acclaimed screenwriter of *A Few Good Men*, *The West Wing*, and *The Social Network*, says it all starts with understanding intention and obstacle. Your protagonist needs to have a clear intention, and there must be a formidable obstacle standing in the way of them getting it. He says that these two essential elements compose the "drive shaft" that creates the friction and tension essential for drama.[4]

These same core elements for dramatic storytelling apply to a good product story. As an innovator, we find something that has thrown life out of balance, and we strive to create a solution to restore the balance. In Matt and Amy's case, they simply wanted to have a smooth pregnancy. Suddenly the condition of preeclampsia emerged to threaten Amy's and their newborn's life. As an innovator, Matt set out to find a way to detect preeclampsia earlier on to better manage the pregnancy and restore that balance. Using Sorkin's model, Matt and Amy's intention was to have a smooth, uneventful pregnancy. Discovering preeclampsia while in labor provided the obstacle in their story.

---

3   Robert McKee, interviewed by Drake Baer, *Fast Company*, October 22, 2013.

4   Aaron Sorkin, *Aaron Sorkin Teaches Screenwriting*, Master Class.

One of the Great Startup Stories of All Time

In his screenplay for *The Social Network*, his movie about the creation of Facebook, Sorkin introduces Mark Zuckerberg as the film's protagonist. Zuckerberg's intention is to create a new social network, and the obstacle is his Harvard classmates, the Winklevoss twins (and their attorneys), who think Mark stole their idea.

Within the overall narrative, Sorkin and director David Fincher also do a tremendous job of introducing the narrative for the innovation itself. Mark had been working on his new social network for some time, but the product story was still fuzzy. In a famous scene, Sorkin and Fincher popularized how Mark might have discovered the essence of the story. Mark literally observed his customer's intention and obstacle during an unexpected conversation with his Harvard classmate Dustin.

Dustin is propped up on a table talking to Mark, who is half ignoring him while pounding away on the keys of a computer in a library. Dustin asks him, "Do you know if Stephanie Addis has a boyfriend?" In the film, Mark Zuckerberg, played by Jesse Eisenberg, is rankled that Dustin is bugging him with this silly question. He barely looks up and says, "No one goes around with a sign on them saying I'm—" Then he stops dead in the middle of the sentence and runs out of the room. Mark races out of the front door of the library, stumbles across the snowy Harvard yard in his flip-flops, and returns to his room to act on his discovery. He immediately adds "relationship status" to the product.

Real or imagined, this scene captures the insight that Mark had about his friend and future customer Dustin, who is the main character in this product story. Mark recognized that Dustin's intention was to get a girlfriend, but he also observed one of the most powerful human emotions in Dustin—fear of rejection. Mark knew it was *way* harder to ask a girl out if she might already have a boyfriend or girlfriend because it would be too embarrassing. That was the obstacle in Dustin's path. Mark solved that problem by giving his customer more information, particularly *this* bit of information. He was confident that the relationship-status feature would help Dustin overcome the obstacle. Mark knew this addition would make the product story complete, so he finished writing the code and pushed the product live to his Harvard classmates.

Every great story has a protagonist whose motivations we fully understand. Likewise, for every innovation there must be a set of customers who benefit from the creation. A deep understanding of the customer and his pain points leads to the precise problem that your innovation will solve.

Mark knew exactly who would use Facebook. He knew what motivated them. He knew what problem he had to solve, and how to solve it. He had a narrative, and it proved to be one of the more compelling inventions of our lifetime.

Who, What, Where, Why, and How

Andrew Stanton, one of the premier writers and directors at Pixar, has perhaps the simplest directive for building stories: "Just make me care." Pixar is in the business of telling stories, and they regularly knock it out of the park. Fourteen of their films have made over half a billion dollars at the box office, and four of those earned over a billion dollars.

To think about structuring a narrative for our product, let's compare it to creating a narrative for one of Pixar's most successful movies. To build this structure we must answer a series of questions: **Who** is the protagonist? **What** are their motivations, and **why** do they feel that way? **What** is the conflict in the story? **How** does it resolve? **Where** does the story take place?

For example, consider the Pixar movie *Toy Story 3*, which is so compelling that it has earned over $1B at the box office. The film begins with a wild chase scene where Woody, the toy cowboy, is in mortal danger on a runaway train. The scene takes place in the mind of Andy, the boy who's played with Woody his whole life. The scene shifts to other flashbacks from Andy's youth: Andy plays with Woody in his highchair; Andy's mom measures her son on the doorjamb, then Andy measures Woody; Woody rides piggyback on Andy's shoulders. Life is good for Andy and great for the toys.

But Andy just turned eighteen, and disaster strikes for the toys. Woody discovers that Andy is going to college. The toys are horror-stricken. Will anyone play with them again? The piggy bank disgustedly says, "Come on! Let's see how much we're goin' for on eBay."

As an audience, we're hooked! We have to know what's going to happen to these toys. Sure, they are animated characters—and just toys—but we care about them. We feel as if we know Woody and his friends. Because human beings are curious, because we've evolved to understand the pattern of a story, we want to know where it's going to go. We're in suspense as passengers on this 103-minute joyride. We don't want to get off!

The protagonist in this story is Woody. Woody, Buzz, and all their toy buddies exist for one reason and one reason only—to be played with. This is their motivation. It's what makes them tick. This is the intention in Sorkin's parlance. There is a rule in musical theater, for example, which is to include an "I want" song that the protagonist must sing in the first twenty minutes of the show. The song lets the audience know whom and what to root for. The *conflict* or obstacle gets established early in the story. Andy, the boy the toys "grew up" with, is leaving for college. Woody and the other toys freak out. As their leader, Woody feels responsible for all the toys. What are they going to do? Who is going to play with them? How will they lead meaningful lives? Woody desperately wants to find a kid to love the toys again. This is the plot imperative, or simply put, what the main character hopes will happen.

The rest of the story, the plot narrative, takes us through the toys' many misadventures as they try to find their way to such a place. The film is set in small-town America where everything seems quaint, friendly, and warm . . . until it isn't! This provides the setting and tone of the film. Rooting for the toys, we anguish over every twist and turn, eager to learn what's going to happen.

Narrative as Innovation Story

To build a strong product strategy, we need a strong innovation story. Let's apply the structure in the Pixar film to that of an innovation story.

I'll use the example of a financial services product created by a bunch of millennial friends called Starbutter AI. Starbutter AI was the new voice assistant for finding financial products developed at UC Berkeley's SkyDeck Accelerator.

The protagonist in a typical narrative structure becomes the customer in our innovation story. The innovator (Starbutter AI in this example) identifies the ideal first target customer and must deeply understand them. Many aspiring entrepreneurs develop a tool, but they haven't figured out yet precisely who's going to use it and why. You can't have a good story without a main character! Ultimately, you want a relatable protagonist to hook your audience so they'll want to hear the entire story.

In Starbutter AI's case, the customer is the millennial looking to build their credit and hopefully become a bit more sophisticated with their finances.

Once we know who the customer is or at least have a hypothesis about an ideal customer, we must get to know them. We must understand their motivations and challenges. In an innovation story, we call these *customer insights*. We need to see how customers think and, more importantly, how they feel.

Starbutter AI's founders spent a lot of time thinking about their customer. Millennials have a remarkable relationship with their phones. I teased my daughter that she thinks she can do everything with her phone. She snapped back, "Well, Dad, that's because I *can!*" The Starbutter AI founders understood this simple fact. They grasped the insight that millennials depend on their phones to solve problems. They love that a simple voice search on their phone will provide a handful of options for them to accomplish any task and make any decision—for example, which rideshare option to select (Uber X or Uber Pool) or even which cupcake to have delivered (peanut butter fudge or strawberry swirl).

But now imagine this same character in our story wants an easy answer from his phone to the question "What credit card should I get?" He cannot find a straightforward answer. Instead, he has to browse websites and comb through myriad sites and volumes of fine print. This is not the experience this customer wants to have.

Now that we know something about the character (customer) and what is on his mind (insights), we can establish the conflict in our innovation story. This is the problem definition. It's where we crisply identify what problem our innovation is going to solve. The tighter the description, the better.

Why can't he simply turn to the phone, answer a few questions, and choose a credit card as if selecting his next cupcake? The Starbutter AI founders had identified the problem they needed to solve. Simply stated: How might we easily find financial services that fit? Starbutter AI's founders suspected that with AI, they could solve this exact problem for this customer.

With the problem clearly in place, we can now articulate to the customer the benefit of solving the problem. It's where we summarize what they want, or more specifically, what they want the product to do for them. In a traditional narrative, this is the plot imperative, or what they get when they achieve their "I want," while in our innovation story, it is the value proposition. This is *not* where we talk about how the product works, but what the product *does* for the customer. For example, the value proposition of this book is in the title: *Get Your Startup Story Straight*.

Starbutter AI's value proposition is simple: Get customized financial recommendations instantly on your phone.

Next you must describe how the product or service works. How does the product deliver the benefit?

Starbutter AI's voice product, which was recognized by Google as the best voice assistant when it launched in 2018, is simple. You ask your phone how to find the right credit card, and Starbutter AI takes over. By asking a few simple questions in your chat window, Starbutter AI uses artificial intelligence to narrow down the best options and serve up just a handful of choices.

It's important to understand how this innovation works in the context of other similar ideas. Someone has probably tried to solve this or a similar problem before. So how is this innovation different and *better* than the other ways people solve the same problem today? We need to position our story in this competitive frame. This is the setting of our product story.

In Starbutter AI's case, the alternative for millennials was to search complicated websites or ask a friend. Neither was particularly compelling to a customer base that wants simple, targeted options delivered to that little device in their pocket.

These are the elements of an innovation narrative. We've used story structure to define our core product strategy in the same way that Pixar built a narrative to create a popular movie. Likewise, Starbutter AI had such a clear story that when they first hit the market, they became the number-one choice in personal finance chat to help young people make important financial choices.

You might be thinking, *Wait a minute, I'm not a professional storyteller. I don't work at Pixar (although that sounds like fun!), and I don't have four years to develop my product story.* If that's what you're thinking, you'd be right. What you need is a simple storytelling framework for your innovation and some straightforward examples of how to apply it.

2

Getting the Story Structure Straight

Is there a simple tool to use to make sure we *have* a story? We need to be confident that it's the *right* story; we must include all the critical story elements; and the pieces need to fit together organically. In short, we need to get the story structure straight. Let's look at Pixar's process and see how they work through it using a basic but effective concept—the storyboard.

Writer-director Andrew Stanton was a major contributor to all four *Toy Story* films, *Finding Dory*, *Monsters Inc.*, and *Wall-E*.

He knows a thing or two about storytelling. Despite his success, he struggled mightily as cowriter and codirector to make *Finding Nemo* work. When Stanton shared an early version of the film with his creative colleagues at Pixar, they identified a big problem. No one liked Marlin, which was problematic since Marlin, Nemo's dad, is the protagonist in the film. The audience should be rooting for Marlin as he goes on his quest to find his captured son, Nemo. Pixar uses a storyboarding process to think through a narrative. They draw every scene like a comic book and stitch the scenes together, ensuring that the characters' motivations are clear, that dramatic tension builds, and that the ending is satisfying. Stanton and his team returned to the storyboards to figure out what needed tweaking. Stanton had advocated for a clever storytelling technique that included a series of flashbacks throughout the film. Pixar's online course, Pixar in a Box, the Art of Storytelling, illustrated this approach by featuring a storyboard with flashback scenes occurring intermittently throughout the film.

As Stanton's team worked to decipher the issue, they developed a hypothesis and tested it. The use of flashbacks had created a problem. There is a crucial flashback scene where a barracuda kills Marlin's wife, Coral, and eats all her eggs except one. Nemo is the only offspring that survives. This scene came at the *end* of the film, which was too late. The storytellers removed the flashbacks altogether and placed the barracuda attack at the beginning of the film. It worked.

Stanton and his team realized that Marlin came across as an overprotective father in the early version of the film, because the audience didn't recognize that Marlin only had Nemo left. Once the audience knew about the barracuda attack at the *beginning* of the story, they empathized with Marlin and started rooting for him. Pixar uses storyboarding to make sure the story works. Their storyboard process allows them to see how the various story elements fit together. They can better assess questions like "Have we clearly established the protagonist in our story?" "Is the main character's intention clear and do we empathize with their circumstance?" "Do we understand what's standing in their way?" "Have we arrived at a satisfying ending?"

Likewise, when you develop a new idea, you should build your own storyboard for your innovation narrative to ensure that you have all the right pieces of your story and that everything adds up. The six frames of our storyboard are

1. the customer (protagonist)

2. customer insights (intention and obstacles)

3. the problem definition (central conflict)

4. the value proposition (aspiration)

5. how the product works (plot)

6. competitive context (setting)

Starting with the protagonist, we will now break down each of these elements so you can create a storyboard for your own concept. You can then vet the story with customers and continue fine-tuning it to make sure it's viable. If something isn't working, keep tweaking the storyboard like the Pixar guys until all the elements fit nicely together.

There are many ways to adjust your storyboard. Perhaps you need to choose a more specific customer segment or identify a richer insight. Perhaps you should define the problem more narrowly. Perhaps you'll want to better illustrate how your idea beats the competitive alternatives.

To improve your ability to frame your own story, we'll go through each element of the storyboard in detail.

Customer (Protagonist)	Insight (Intention and Obstacles)	Problem Definition (Central Conflict)
1 ————————	**2** ————————	**3** ————————
Value Proposition (Aspiration)	How It Works (Plot)	Competitive Context (Setting)
4 ————————	**5** ————————	**6** ————————

Storyboard Element #1: Customer (Protagonist)

The protagonist anchors every story, and likewise, the customer grounds every innovation narrative. Some innovations start with the discovery of a new technology or science, but to create a successful product, the innovator must eventually identify the customer who will want and use that technology. You can then tailor the technology to meet that customer's needs. The product folks at Air New Zealand (ANZ) discovered this when they rethought the protagonist in their story.

Have you ever flown over an ocean with young kids in tow? Ask anyone who has tried it; it's no walk in the park. Air New Zealand never thought about this problem, even though most of their flights are long-haul flights over oceans.

That changed around 2009 when they hired innovation firm IDEO to help them rethink their design process. Until that point, ANZ always organized their customers based on their ability to pay—economy, business, or first class. So IDEO helped ANZ think of their customers as different types of *people*. They created specific personas by starting to think of their customers as families with young children and newly married couples. It was much easier to innovate once they had a more explicit protagonist for their *new* product story.

The airline talked to moms and dads and learned how challenging it was to wrangle their children during a long flight. They brought actors into a design lab—these actors also had families and experience flying long flights—and the design team heard and observed just how hard this experience was for people with young families. The pain in their voices was palpable as they spoke about their frustrations. Their children would get restless; they'd want to play games or stretch out and sleep. These things were impossible to accommodate on regular coach seats. Air New Zealand developed a *new* narrative around this *new* protagonist.

They arrived at the Air New Zealand Economy Sky Couch. The Sky Couch is a row of three adjoining seats with leg rests that move up to form a couch. Families could stretch out with their kids, play games, and take naps for the price of three coach tickets they would have bought anyway. The Sky Couch won a Best Economy Class Innovation award from *Travel and Leisure*. And the families regained their sanity.

Which Protagonist to Choose?

Many innovators face a different challenge in finding their protagonists. They wonder, "Who do I feature as the main character in my story? What if the person who buys the product is not the same person who receives the greatest benefit from it?" If you're creating an ed-tech solution for young people, for example, do you tell the story through the lens of the child or the parent? If you've got a technology that makes emergency room doctors more productive, do you tell the story through the doctor's lens or the hospital administrator who makes the purchase decision?

Iris Wedeking is CEO and cofounder of iDentical, a drill-free dental implant solution. It's an early-stage company that was part of Berkeley's SkyDeck Accelerator in the fall of 2019. In prepping for her "Demo Day" pitch, Iris faced a choice. Should she choose the patient or the dentist as the customer in her story? The patient is the ultimate beneficiary of iDentical's custom dental implant solution, but the dentist buys her product.

Featuring the person who has the greatest pain—and the most to gain—is simplest. Remember, we are using the story to make the listener care about the protagonist. You can always introduce additional characters as the story evolves, but it's best to build the core narrative around whoever suffers more. That customer will benefit most by your innovation, and it will likely make for a more engaging and compelling story.

Iris pursued this strategy by talking about the patient. She made it even more personal (and painful) by saying that most people will need replacement teeth in their lifetime. In fact, most people will have *many* teeth replaced. Then Iris played the recorded sound of a dentist's drill. Six hundred investors and tech enthusiasts simultaneously squirmed in their seats. Iris then described what is typically required for a patient to get a tooth replaced. It takes almost a year to get your replacement tooth, because the process involves a long waiting period before you can get your implant. Once you get in the chair, you can expect quite a bit of drilling. It's expensive, too, because your family dentist typically isn't equipped to pull it off.

Iris then described a better, simpler solution: iDentical. The family dentist removes the patient's old tooth, scans it, and then sends the scan to iDentical. iDentical uses the scan to design and manufacture a personalized replacement tooth, which is the implant. The implant is then shipped back to your family dentist, who places it in the patient's mouth within a week or two of extraction. Ta-da. Further into the presentation, Iris talked about how the dentist benefits as well. The dentist now has a new revenue stream and happier patients. Win-win! And the sound of that drill is about all we need to feel the customer's pain!

Some decisions concerning choosing the protagonist prove even more complicated. People selling medical devices, for example, may choose to target hospital administrators who buy the products for their doctors, who, in turn, use them for the benefit of their patients. There are three different potential protagonists from which to choose. We see this pattern in many business-to-business (B2B) examples. Again, the same rule applies. The story of the person suffering the most is likely the richest one to tell.

Finally, we have the case of the two-sided market—a "love story." eBay is a classic example because its platform meets both the seller's and the buyer's needs. We need to understand both characters in the story to see why they are meant to be together. I'll delve into this narrative in more depth in Act 3.

Storyboard Element #2: Customer Insights (Intention and Obstacles)

The best innovations address a deeply felt insight. The greater the pain, the greater the opportunity for gain. The pain points form the basis for the problem you plan to solve. But how do you uncover what is truly bugging the customer to determine what they really want?

Why, Why, Why?

A good place to start is by talking to prospective customers. Lots of them. Startup guru Steve Blank employs the lean startup methodology in his classes and famously insists that innovators "get out of the building" and speak with one hundred customers. Be prepared to dig like a journalist, detective, or anthropologist. It's useful to employ the Three Whys approach. Ask why the customer feels a certain way. Then ask, "Why is that?" And finally, ask, "And why is *that?*" Three Whys. Feel free to keep going. Sometimes the answers validate your initial hypothesis, but often they lead you in a completely different direction. This process of discovering real insights is one of the most important skills an innovator can develop. If you want to go deep on the subject, read Steve Portigal's *Interviewing Users* or Giff Constable's *Talking to Humans.*

A recent commercial from a packaged goods company demonstrates the importance of the Three Whys better than any textbook ever could. It begins with a floppy-haired teenage boy stepping up to the counter at the Department of Motor Vehicles (DMV) office and stating, "Hi, I want to apply for a driver's license." The DMV worker, a middle-aged, seen-it-all woman behind the counter, stares at him flatly and says, "What do you really want?" He is a bit surprised, smiles (as if to say, "Well, duh!"), and answers, "To be able to drive a car." She doesn't budge: "What do you really, *really* want?" The teen is now trying to figure out where this is going and replies, "I want my independence?" She continues, "What do you really, really, *really* want?" Now he's got it. He says, "To show my parents that I can solve my own problems—that I don't *want* their help." He's now practically shouting. "The truth is that they need me more than I need them!" She isn't satisfied yet: "What do you really, really, really, *really* want?" And finally, exasperated, he shouts, "I want Reese's Puffs, OK?" Satisfied that she's found the real reason, she matter-of-factly states, "OK," and slides a bowl of Reese's Puffs cereal over to him. "Thank you," he says. "Next!" she yells. And then the title card comes onscreen, which reads, "Reese's Puffs cereal: It's what you really, really, really, really want." Perfect.

When you discover the deep-seated motivation behind your customer, it often opens new doors for telling the story, but it's equally helpful for informing what to build in the first place.

Baby Shaming

Good consumer researchers operate like the lady at the DMV. They see themselves as investigators. But the researchers that Kimberly-Clark hired to observe young parents must have felt like therapists.

Kimberly-Clark had always innovated in their Huggies diaper business by focusing on technology. They consistently explored ways to create materials that wick away moisture more efficiently.

But to understand their customers even better, they sent ethnographic researchers into their homes to see if they were missing anything. They observed the young parents, listened to them, and asked many questions. They asked about their lives with young children. They asked about what they liked and didn't like about the diapers they used. And they inquired about the experience of changing diapers.

Smart researchers know to ask one last question before ending an interview. "Is there anything else you'd like to tell me?" Parents from one stage of parenthood—those potty training their kids—shared a common lament. They answered, "You know what I hate? I hate it when our friends look at us and say, 'Oh, your kids are still in diapers?'" Who passes judgment on a baby?! In fact, they were judging the parents! Regardless, this snide remark truly set them off.

After hearing this frustration over and over, Kimberly-Clark had an epiphany. For this type of customer whose children were still potty training, they needed to create a diaper that was more like clothing. The researchers were trying, in the language of anthropology, to find real meaning here. They determined that the primary issue was how parents felt they were being perceived. This insight inspired the creation of Huggies Pull-Ups, a diaper that pulls up like underwear. The Pull-Ups business is now a huge driver of the Huggies franchise. And this innovation would never have happened if the company hadn't left the building and gone into the homes of their customers to find out what really, really, really, *really* drove them crazy.

The Business Based on an Insight Rooted in Culture

Diishan Imira grew up in Oakland, California, with an entrepreneurial drive. As a young man, he explored different business ideas and struggled to get something off the ground. Why? He hadn't discovered the right problem to solve. Writers often hear, "Write what you know." A similar mantra applies to entrepreneurs: "If you experience—or see—something that's broken, fix it." Diishan did exactly that.

Diishan is Black and has several family members who are hairstylists participating in the huge $6B US hair extensions business. Diishan noticed that the stylists missed out on a considerable part of the value chain in the industry; they never made a penny on the sale of the hair itself. They were only paid for braiding the extensions into their customers' hair.

Previously, a Black woman who wanted braids or hair extensions would have to travel to a retail outlet to buy the hair. This meant an extra step for the customer. Furthermore, the stylist, who was typically Black, didn't make any money on the transaction. The stores were run mainly by Korean Americans, who built a thriving industry in the 1960s as an outgrowth of a successful Korean wig industry. This business took off for Koreans in the mid-'60s after the US barred Chinese hair from imported wigs. Koreans cornered the wig market, and Korean immigrants to America built a hugely successful retail trade. Diishan had no issue with this success story, but he felt that some of that value should come back into the Black community. He also thought he could improve the consumer experience. Inspired by these insights, he started Mayvenn.

Mayvenn, a platform that connects customers and stylists, enables the stylist to profit from the sale of the hair itself. The customer goes to Mayvenn.com and picks out the hair of their choice. They then select a local stylist in Mayvenn's network to "install" the hair for free. Mayvenn baked the price of the install into the hair. Now the stylist gets traffic from Mayvenn and a percentage of the value of the sale of the hair. Diishan brought ownership back to the Black community and tapped into the important cultural notion of supporting your own.

To get his business funded, Diishan had to find Silicon Valley investors who grasped the opportunity. Diishan identified the insights about his customers' frustrations so well that some venture people saw the potential value immediately. He and a few visionary investors drove across the Bay to Oakland to meet these stylists and hear their frustrations firsthand. Diishan eventually raised $23M to build and grow the business and attracted fifty thousand stylists. His investors include 500 Startups, Launch Capital, Andreessen Horowitz, and Serena Williams.

Find the Emotional Need as Well as the Functional One

One of my mentors in the San Francisco ad business was a thoughtful dynamo named Steve Darland, who once told me, "Our greatest human failing is that we forget what we're doing." Great innovators usually don't suffer from this problem. When they wake up every morning, they know exactly what to do. They know who their customer is, what's driving them mad, and what problem they are trying to solve. They work every day on fixing it.

My colleague Dr. Sara Beckman talks about identifying the different jobs a product has. There are functional jobs as well as social and emotional ones. Before you get to the problem, you need to understand your customer's functional, social, and emotional needs.

The best innovators know their story—especially what's at the heart of the story—and so does everyone on their team.

Twenty-two years ago, the folks at Research in Motion (RIM) created the Blackberry, an extraordinary innovation that transformed the mobile communications business. RIM's success resulted from its laser focus on solving a problem that no one else had been able to tackle.

The first time I saw the Blackberry in its native habitat was in the hands of a C-level executive in 2000 in a cab in New York. I was riding with Jon, an old college buddy who ran a digital news startup at the time. He was the guy who gave his speech immediately before me at our graduation. When I saw him pull this strange device out of his pocket, I exclaimed, "What's that?"

Like most senior execs, Jon was either visiting customers or sitting in meetings from 8 a.m. to 6 p.m. This work style had many drawbacks, but the biggest problem was keeping up with what was going on. Like me, Jon is old enough to have started his career *before* email. Imagine reading actual paper memos that you took home every night in a big manila folder.

By 2000, however, every businessperson communicated by email. These emails flew around while Jon sat in meetings all day. Imagine how he felt. He was the boss. He was in charge. But from 8 a.m. to 6 p.m., he had no idea what was happening. He felt left out, uninformed—out of control. He desperately wanted to stay in touch and be kept apprised throughout the day. His functional need was to get his email wherever he happened to be. His emotional need was to be in the know at all times so he could feel in control, and the social need was to project to others that he was in charge.

Remarkably, no one had solved this problem until RIM grabbed hold of this story. RIM's job was to keep people like Jon connected to their business messages wherever they were. The solution was a seamless mobile email solution. RIM built the first Blackberry in 1999 and tweaked it in early 2000.

The device had a large display, a QWERTY keyboard, a scroll wheel, and push service. Well, no one had such a clear narrative up until this point. No one really understood this insight—both functional and emotional—about how desperate the C-level exec was to be in the loop. No one else made it happen. RIM saw the need and built a compelling technology that played nicely within the enterprise infrastructure, and they completely dominated the market for most of the next decade.

One of my former students, Ehsan Hoque, who recently joined the Amazon Prime Video product team, relayed a great story to me about valuing customer centricity. During Ehsan's orientation session on his very first day, he learned a famous company story that is now baked into Amazon lore. In the early days of the company, Jeff Bezos heard a comment in a meeting that irked him. Without saying anything, he suddenly jumped from his chair and left the room. His colleagues were baffled. When he returned, he brought an empty chair into the room, which he rolled right up to the table. He told the group that they weren't thinking about things from the customer perspective and that this empty chair would now represent the customer. In every meeting thereafter, Bezos insisted on reserving an empty chair at the table so his teams would consider the customer in every key decision. This is a brilliant tactic, and it's obviously proved incredibly successful for Amazon. That said, it's not enough to simply keep the customer in mind. Rather, it's essential to truly understand them. Ask them thoughtful questions and keep digging until you discover what makes them tick. Determine their functional and emotional needs. Once you've gathered and distilled rich insights about your customer, you can move on to figure out exactly what problem to solve to help improve their life.

Storyboard Element #3: Problem Definition (Central Conflict)

Innovators can learn a lot from the personal stories of individuals overcoming seemingly impossible obstacles to achieve greatness. Some of our greatest stories are tales of the hero's journey. Whether it's the incomparable narrative of Nelson Mandela changing the course of South African history after spending twenty-seven years in jail, or the story of Ruth Bader Ginsburg, one of only nine women in her

Harvard Law School class of five hundred, eventually becoming a beloved United States Supreme Court justice, major obstacles stood in their way. In a 2015 interview in the *New York Times*, Ginsburg said that she had three strikes against her: "First I was Jewish. Wall Street firms were just beginning to accept Jews. Then I was a woman. But the killer was my daughter, Jane, who was four by then." Great accomplishments typically involve our hero overcoming seemingly impossible impediments. To understand these stories is to appreciate the importance of the role of conflict in our narrative structure.

The Little Black Boy Who Wouldn't Leave the Library

In 1959, a nine-year-old Black child, Ron McNair, hiked a mile across town to borrow some library books. The problem was that Ron grew up in Lake City, South Carolina, where the Jim Crow South was alive and well. When little Ron approached the counter with his books, the librarian said, "This library is not for coloreds. If you don't leave, I'm going to call the police." Ron faced a real challenge. Did he turn around and walk home empty-handed, or did he stand up for what was right? Ron propped himself up on the counter and said he'd wait. The police arrived and so did Ron's mom, praying that her son would be OK. To their credit, the police convinced the librarian that this wasn't a travesty and had her lend the books to Ron.

Ron's brother Carl shared this story with StoryCorps, which preserves American stories. Through books, Ron McNair developed a love of stories and science. Later, while watching *Star Trek* as a teen, his brother Carl noted that Ron said he'd like to be on a spaceship one day. Carl told Ron that a Black person on a spaceship was science fiction, but Carl explains now, "You know . . . to Ron, it was science possibility." Once again, Ron faced an obstacle and was determined to overcome it.

Ron McNair eventually did become an astronaut and tragically was one of the seven people killed in the space shuttle *Challenger* disaster in 1986. He was thirty-five. Twenty-five years to the day after his death, that Lake City library was renamed the Ronald E. McNair Life History Center.

This story illustrates the next part of our narrative—conflict. Ron confronted more than one obstacle that seemed insurmountable, but with persistence and self-belief, he overcame them. He faced the extreme challenge of changing attitudes about Black people and ultimately did so by pursuing his passion for science.

The Google Goose That Laid the Golden Egg

In an innovation narrative, we need to identify the conflict in our story, which takes the form of the exact problem the customer hopes to overcome. Once we understand that barrier, we can turn it into a clear—and specific—problem definition for the innovator to solve. We know in what direction to head in order to solve it. In a design-thinking process, we refer to this as the "how might we" statement.

One of the most popular tech products in our life provides an example. When Google created AdWords in 2000, they set out to solve the age-old problem facing advertisers, best captured by the nineteenth- and early-twentieth-century merchant John Wanamaker. "Half the money I spend on advertising is wasted," he famously said. "The trouble is I don't know which half." Wanamaker was referring to the challenge of targeting ads to the people who might be interested in his products. Until relatively recently, this has been extremely hard to do. Google, which had just introduced their powerful consumer search tool, knew the problem they needed to solve for businesses: "How might we create an efficient way for advertisers to find—and engage with—the most likely customers for their products?"

By creating a self-service platform for advertisers to connect with individuals searching for keywords online, Google took what the Yellow Pages started decades earlier and made it exponentially better. Google AdWords directly matched companies with the people who were searching expressly for the products they sold. For example, when a person is searching for a place to stay in Manuel Antonio, Costa Rica, the hotels that operate in that town will be highly motivated to connect with them. Who could possibly be a better prospect for one of these hotels than someone who is expressing their intent through this search term? Google identified that problem and solved it. They built a platform that lets businesses bid for search terms so that if the business pays enough, its ad will appear above the natural search results for that term. With a clear problem definition and passionate, creative people, anything is possible.

Pick the Right Problem

One of the most significant challenges for the innovator is framing the problem. If framed too broadly, it's hard to know where to start to create a minimum viable product (MVP) that effectively solves the problem. But if the problem is framed too narrowly, it might limit the power of the solution. There's a concept called ladder of abstraction, which we can use to determine the proper scope. The innovator explores a series of questions to create a range of problem statements, from the too abstract to the overly concrete, and then settles on the one they feel they should solve. We move up the ladder of abstraction by asking the question, "Why is this important?" We move down the ladder by asking, "What's stopping you?" In this way, we can craft the right-sized problem statement.

In an alternative universe, using the AdWords example, the Google team might have attacked a more abstract problem, such as how they could help advertisers get new customers, or they might have tried to solve a narrower problem, such as how they could match the single best customer with the ideal seller. Although this solution would deliver results, it would be too limiting.

But Google landed on figuring out how to create an efficient way for advertisers to find and engage with the most likely customers for their products. By exploring a range of problem statements, the innovator can focus on the part of the problem they're most interested in and most capable of solving.

The Unfocused Problem Statement: A Common Stumbling Block for Innovators

Albert Einstein allegedly said, "If I had an hour to solve a problem, I'd spend fifty-five minutes thinking about the problem and five minutes thinking about solutions." In my work with innovators, I've found far too many who need to spend more time on problem framing. One of my students, Will, recently shared a product narrative for a new app for backpackers traveling in a foreign country. He had many useful insights about the backpacker's desire to travel like a local, but instead of a single problem statement, he had three.

1. How might we let backpackers communicate with locals if they don't speak local languages?

2. How might we let backpackers know what locals do and where they go in real life?

3. How might we make solo backpackers feel safe while exploring new places and things?

That's a lot to tackle. I encouraged Will to focus on a single statement built on his insights that would create a problem specific enough that he'd have a chance to solve it. He landed on "How might we enable foreign travelers to have a more authentic and safe experience?" This statement narrowed Will's focus and provided crisp direction for building his MVP.

The challenge facing the innovator in clarifying her problem statement is comparable to the challenge facing an author in crafting a clear conflict in her story. The clearer the conflict, the easier it is for the audience to follow the story and root for the hero. Returning to our *Finding Nemo* example, the conflict in the story came when Nemo was snatched away by a diver, and the protagonist, Marlin, had to find his only child in a vast ocean and safely deliver him home. It was easy to build the story from there. Likewise, for the innovator, the clearer the problem statement she creates, the more directed she'll be in building the solution.

Storyboard Element #4: Value Proposition (Aspiration)

In a narrative, a character aspires to some outcome. We follow a story to see if the protagonist gets what they want. Likewise, in an innovation narrative, we need to understand the benefit that the customer will experience from our innovation. We call this benefit the *value proposition*. Here's the story of a powerful value proposition from an inspired innovator.

Look Ma, No Hands

Great value propositions immediately telegraph to the user why they should care about a new innovation. Google's Home Hub is a fantastic product that has several features. It's a large display designed for home use in the kitchen or garage, with a full-range speaker and the ability to control the device by voice. That's what it *is*. But what it *does* for the user is something else—that's the value proposition. To derive a strong value proposition, I suggest that innovators try to complete one of the following sentences: "Now I can . . . " or "Now I can have . . ." There's something you couldn't do before, but now you can.

In a commercial touting the product, Google shows several home videos of people in the kitchen who desperately need to have their hands free to cook but also need to interact with their phone. While watching a cooking demonstration on their little device, a budding chef finds himself trying to answer a call while his hands are covered in dough. Another watches a slow cooker overflow onto the counter, thus dousing the phone in a stew. In a third scenario, a baker drops their device in the KitchenAid mixer, and it spins around wildly inside. The ad does a great job of teasing the problem that the Google Home Hub solves.

Imagine trying to make ravioli from scratch while watching a YouTube demo. Your hands move in and out of the flour, the finished dough, and the pork filling. You need to start the video at a critical point in the process. You really don't want to wash your hands at every step; rather, you desperately wish you could get hands-free help. You want to start a video with just your voice. Google Home Hub delivers exactly that! Alexa or Siri might explain the process, but only Google Home Hub shows you.

"Hands-free help" is the value proposition. It's the benefit to the user; in other words, there is something that they can do now that they couldn't do before.

That's why the customer should care about this product and why they should read further or listen to more of the story. Google captures this benefit with the tagline "Help at a glance."

An Elephant Never Forgets

Some of the greatest taglines are calls to action inspired by the value proposition. The two most famous are "Think Different" (Apple) and "Just Do It" (Nike).

If you keep your eyes open, you'll stumble across great examples wherever you look. When the note-taking app Evernote was launched, their tagline was "Remember Everything." Their symbol is the elephant, because of the old saying that an elephant never forgets. We always forget things that we hear or learn, so who wouldn't want to remember everything? It's a compelling value proposition and tagline all in one. In Zendesk's early days, when the company was building a customer base, its value proposition was "Have a better relationship with your customer." Zendesk's help desk software let businesses do just that. It was clear and effective. Wootric, a customer engagement platform, led with its value proposition "Win customers for life" to attract their own customers that they hoped to lock in for life.

The greatest challenge for innovators building their storyboards is crafting a succinct value proposition. Creators would rather list a string of benefits than find a pithy, memorable, single statement of value. But a great value proposition is like catnip. It intrigues the prospective customer. It gets them excited. Once they hear the value proposition, they want to learn more. They wonder, "Wow, I can get *that*? Awesome! How do they do it? How does it work?" The prospect is hooked, and they want to learn more. "I can get hands-free help in the kitchen? Great! Tell me more about Google Home Hub." "I can remember everything? Great, I need that! I've got to learn more about how Evernote works."

Storyboard Element #5: How the Product Works (Plot)

The plot of any story takes us through the steps the character takes to overcome obstacles and get what they want. In our innovation story, it's tantamount to the product or service itself. What exactly is the product or program? How does it work? How does it address the specific issues you identified in getting to know your customer? In the following story about a young innovator in the economic development sector, I'll distinguish between the plot of the origin story and the plot of the customer story.

Sasha's Summer in South Sudan

Sasha Fisher is a young woman with grand ambitions. As a twenty-year-old college student, Sasha was a summer volunteer in South

Sudan when she was struck by the number of development projects she came across that had slid into disrepair, such as unused schools and broken water wells. She set off on a journey to ascertain the root cause of the problem.

As she explored the problem, she discovered that the projects had been conceived and built by outside development organizations. They came in, built the facilities, and left. The residents had no buy-in and didn't have the capability or commitment to maintain them. Sasha created the nonprofit organization Spark Microgrants to solve this problem. In a short time, Sasha raised $200,000, targeted communities in East Africa, and directed the funds to initiatives that affected over twenty thousand lives.

This is Sasha's origin story. She tells it to convey what inspired her to create Spark Microgrants. Let's compare that to the customer narrative and the plot of the customer's story.

The customer narrative begins with the villagers in Uganda, Rwanda, and Burundi, where Spark Microgrants operates. These are the protagonists in the product story. Consistent with Sasha's earlier discovery in South Sudan, the villagers in these three East African countries wanted to be involved in development projects in their communities. They wanted to select which projects to take on and then be empowered to make them happen. The beginning of this customer narrative is now in place (customer, motivation, and problem definition), which means it's time to introduce the solution or the plot of the story.

Spark Microgrants is a different kind of development initiative. Spark Microgrants' platform does three things:

1. empowers communities to determine which projects to take on,

2. enables the residents to be involved in the construction themselves, and

3. includes a crowd-funding mechanism to allow people anywhere to donate to specific Spark projects.

Rule of Three

We've now explained what the product is and how it works. It's best to use the "rule of three" when summarizing what your product does. There's only so much information a listener can retain. If you can explain your product simply—in three points—your audience should be able to recall how your product works.

There's an art to telling this part of your product story simply. Think about what your customer must know about how your solution works, and bring that information forward. For example, imagine that you found a better way to help someone buy a used car. Shift is a new company that promises to "Skip the headaches of used car buying." The folks at Shift know that their customers might be thinking about three key steps: "I need to find a better car, then sell my old one, and somehow figure out how to pay for it." Shift summarizes the "how it works" this way:

1. Shop cars: Browse thousands of cars online and test drive from home.

2. Sell or trade in: Find out your car's value in minutes.

3. Finance: Get personalized terms, no obligations.

Our goal as a storyteller is to tease just enough information so your audience can easily assemble a picture in their mind of how you are solving the messy problem you said you could solve. Once you've described this perfect solution, now all you need to do is be sure that you've conveyed how the mousetrap you built is better than all the other ones out there.

Storyboard Element #6: Competitive Context (Setting)

Every story takes place in a setting that creates a world of context for the narrative. For example, *Slumdog Millionaire* takes place in a crowded, complex urban environment in Mumbai. *Coco* takes place in a little Mexican village. *Field of Dreams* takes place in an Iowa cornfield. These unique and vivid settings inform each of these films, including the type of people who live there, the lives they lead, and what they value.

Likewise, every innovation narrative takes place in a setting. No innovation exists in a vacuum. The setting for your innovation is its competitive context. How are people solving the problem today? What do they like about the current solutions? What bugs them? Who are your competitors, and how is your idea different *and better* than the alternatives? Following is one such innovation story that also, like *Slumdog*, takes place in a crowded setting.

Tribes Need to Be Fed

Imagine a scenario where you and a few buddies get together and decide to create a new website to take on ESPN, Yahoo! Sports, and every local sports site to boot, but your site will be expressly for the *most* passionate sports fans. This sounds like a scenario where there'd be lots of drinking involved and not much critical thinking. Despite being surprisingly sober, that's exactly what David Finocchio, Alexander Freund, Bryan Goldberg, and David Nemetz did in 2007 when they created Bleacher Report or BR.

These guys knew they had to do something different to stand out. So, they capitalized on an unmet need among their fellow sports fans to carve out a valuable niche for themselves. *Fan* is short for *fanatic*. Groups of fans form tribes of fanatics, and they simply can't get enough information about their teams.

The BR guys also knew that there weren't enough professional writers to populate a site with the depth of content their audience craved. So they turned to the fans themselves, empowering them to write about their teams. BR created a platform where fans could create and post articles. They made it easy for the best-read amateur writers to surface and build reputations of their own. The result was a site that was continually posting new content about a fan's teams, which fulfilled their passion for a constant flow of news about their squad.

To visualize your competitive position in the setting for your product, create a competitive map. Build a two-by-two grid with one dimension on the north-south axis and another on the east-west axis. Place the competitors on the map, so your product resides in the upper right-hand corner (the +/+ quadrant). In Bleacher Report's case, one axis was for general vs. local coverage, and the other was for professionally created content vs. fan-sourced content. BR sat alone in the upper right-hand corner as the *only* sports website with fan-created, local content on every team. Why? Because they addressed an unmet customer need—giving fans more content about their teams.

Bleacher Report kept growing until the big guys had to take them seriously. In 2012, Turner Sports bought the startup for over $170M. Not bad for an idea that sounded as if it resulted from a late-night bender in a sports bar.

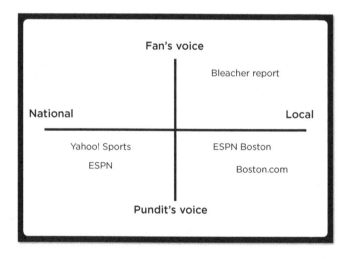

Haven't I Met You Before?

Bleacher Report is not alone. Sonder, a new hospitality solution that redefines the hotel experience, had a big challenge in positioning their product vis-à-vis their competitors. On an early version of their website, they led with the copy "Local Flavor Meets Hotel Comforts." Their "about" copy read, "With Sonder, you can live like a local and enjoy the convenience and consistency of a hotel. Sonders come in all shapes and sizes, from airy urban lofts to rustic seaside cottages." At this point the reader is likely thinking, *I use Airbnb. Why do I need this new thing?* This is what our brain naturally does. It seeks out familiar reference points when we hear about something new. It's as if the reader is thinking, *Haven't I met you before?* If you are the folks at Sonder, you have to recognize this and tackle this challenge head-on.

It's incumbent on Sonder then to acknowledge this context and be extremely clear about what makes them different. The founders of Sonder realized that some travelers liked the idea of staying in a cool place in a charming neighborhood, but they couldn't get over their fear of the unknowns. Will the sheets and towels be clean and bug free? Will there be someone to turn to if I have a question? Will I have the amenities that I'm used to at a hotel, like Wi-Fi and a coffee machine?

The copy on their website went on to say, "But inside each one, you'll find the same crisp white linens, quality standards, and concierge service." Now when you go to Sonder's website, they go even further. They list amenities that include electronic self-check-in, a comfort foam mattress, 24/7 customer support, a fully equipped kitchen, bath essentials, artisan coffee, water, and so on. Sonder knows they must acknowledge the setting of this story—a world where Airbnb, VRBO, and hotels already exist—and really distinguish themselves if they are going to gain market traction. It looks as though they've started to do so, with operations now in over thirty cities and seven countries. Sonder recently raised $210M at a valuation of over $1B and is expected to go public at a valuation over $2B. They've clearly convinced investors that they have carved out a viable place in the market.

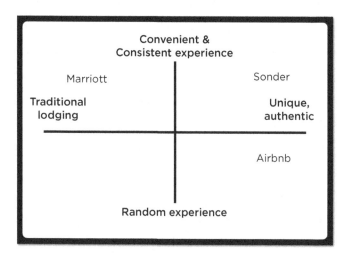

Bleacher Report and Sonder are examples of new companies in crowded categories that had to work especially hard to build narratives that stood out. They realized they had to find a specific segment for whom they could provide a better solution. In BR's case, it was intensely loyal local sports fans. For Sonder, it was travelers looking for a neighborhood vibe and a little extra comfort.

Another category that's about as crowded as a crosswalk in Shibuya is the social media space. When a group of innovators came up with the Marco Polo app, they built their point of distinction right into their value proposition statement: "Stay in touch with the people who matter most to you." The implied message in that statement is that most of the people with whom you are communicating on social media don't *really* matter to you. Their story goes on to say, "Unlike social media, there is no wasted time, no social comparisons, and no likes! Connect with the most important people in your life, not the entire world." Their solution, which allows users to send asynchronous video messages to close friends and family members, isn't for everybody, but it beats the alternatives for certain customers in certain cases. Marco Polo acknowledges the context of the alternative solutions in their category and makes certain to amplify what makes their app special. Make sure you are able to frame your category, and your position in it, in a way that allows you to do the same.

3

Putting It All Together: The Innovation Narrative

Now here's a story that illustrates all six elements coming together for one great narrative. I met the entrepreneur Pranoti Nagarkar in 2009 while serving as a judge at the Berkeley-Intel Global Challenge, a competition for entrepreneurs from sixty countries. Pranoti is an Indian expat engineer living in Singapore. In her pitch, she told a compelling narrative.

She described a fascinating insight about her generation of Indian expat families, or Non-Resident Indians (NRIs), where both parents are working professionals. They were feeling guilty. The guilt came from their busy lifestyles and the difficulty of not having the time to share certain aspects of their culture with their children.

Pranoti recalled her own experience growing up, spending time in the kitchen with her mom, who would cook traditional meals and tell stories. Now as a full-time working professional, Pranoti could no longer prepare all the foods that Indian families ate for generations, and she felt that her children were missing out. Pranoti knew that she couldn't make the guilt go away entirely, but as a smart entrepreneur, she identified a very specific problem she could solve. She took on the roti problem.

A staple of the Indian diet, roti is a flatbread that can take anywhere from thirty minutes to an hour to make. Pranoti noted that 2.3 billion rotis are eaten *every* day worldwide. And there's no alternative other than ordering out or serving frozen rotis, which by all accounts are nowhere near as tasty. Pranoti's solution was to create the Rotimatic. We saw a demo back in 2009, and it was clunky, but it worked. After a long day on the job, a parent could come home and simply put flour and water in a machine, and in ninety seconds out popped a delicious roti. Pranoti's team won third place in that global competition, and after five years of development, they launched the Rotimatic. The product typically sells for $1,000, and it's often on back order because it is so popular.

This innovation narrative has all the same elements as those you'd find in a book or movie. The protagonist (the customer) is the modern Non-Resident Indian parent. The character's motivation (or customer insight) is to assuage their guilt stemming from not giving their children the same cultural experiences they had. The story conflict (problem definition) is about how hard it is for these exhausted working parents to create such a central part of the evening meal. In the parlance of design-thinking language, we might word the problem statement like this: "How might we make it easy to bake healthy roti?" The character's aspiration (value proposition) is to connect with their culture and enjoy fresh roti in minutes! The plot (the product) is the Rotimatic itself. The Rotimatic is made up of

1. AI and IOT that optimizes roti making over time,

2. a fine-particle dispenser that precisely calculates ingredients, and

3. custom-designed heat flow to cook the roti from the inside.

And finally, we have the context for the story. How is the customer solving the problem today? The current alternatives for the customer are

1. working less to spend more time in the kitchen,

2. frozen roti, or

3. take-out food.

Together, these elements compose the innovation narrative.

Let's go back to our innovation narrative storyboard framework and put all these elements together.

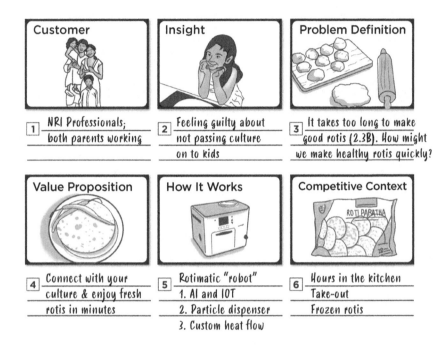

Customer	Insight	Problem Definition
1 NRI Professionals; both parents working	**2** Feeling guilty about not passing culture on to kids	**3** It takes too long to make good rotis (2.3B). How might we make healthy rotis quickly?

Value Proposition	How It Works	Competitive Context
4 Connect with your culture & enjoy fresh rotis in minutes	**5** Rotimatic "robot" 1. AI and IOT 2. Particle dispenser 3. Custom heat flow	**6** Hours in the kitchen Take-out Frozen rotis

This is a favorite product story of mine because of how it resonates with my Non-Resident Indian students. The vast majority know of someone who has a Rotimatic or have one themselves. One student told me that she just completed a text exchange the day before with her husband that ended with "We have to get a Rotimatic." She explained that their lives were so out of control they needed something to ground them and connect them—and their children—with their culture. Not only was Pranoti tapping into a functional need (fresh rotis, quickly), but she also uncovered an emotional need (preserving a cultural connection). This value proposition was so powerful that it drove rapid adoption despite the extravagant expense.

The innovation narrative storyboard that we've built in the past two chapters becomes foundational to everything that follows. It informs who we're targeting in our go-to-market strategy, it provides clear direction to our product and engineering teams that are building the solution, and of course it provides the narrative backbone for all of our storytelling in every medium. As I'll explain further in the next section, this storyboard is the strategic backbone for your innovation. You must regularly reassess and refine it to ensure that your story elements reflect everything you've learned from your customer and competitors as you bring your idea to the world.

Story as Strategy

The Rotimatic example demonstrates the power of having a solid story in place before going too far down the product development path. The Rotimatic may not have been the right product for Indian people living in India, but for those Indians living far from home, it helped satisfy their craving for a stronger connection to their culture. Pranoti knew from other Non-Resident Indian friends and neighbors in Singapore that the product would be compelling if she could build it.

A well-crafted product story is a strategic tool to support you early in the product development process. Consider my experience with Anuj Gupta at Berkeley's SkyDeck Accelerator, where I've collaborated with hundreds of entrepreneurs.

"Should I speak with the customer?" Anuj asked about half-way through our advising session. "Yes!" I practically shouted, even though Anuj was sitting about three feet away on a cool, office-of-the-future modular bench straight out of a *Black Mirror* episode. Anuj was working on a product *without* having a clear-minded focus on who his customer was or what issues she might face. We were experiencing a crystal-clear example of why understanding story is fundamental to developing a product strategy. I asked, "How can you possibly build a useful product without understanding who's going to use it and why?"

Anuj and his colleagues had spent several years developing mapping software to process information for the driverless car industry. But Anuj and his cofounders became frustrated with the pace of development in this field. They pivoted to a more immediate business opportunity with the creation of Go360io, a subscription-based ride-hailing service. Anuj speculated that the technology they'd developed could support a subscription-based alternative to Uber or Lyft. He just hadn't checked in with anyone yet to see if they needed it.

The power of understanding story framework is that it *forces* the innovator to think about the protagonist in their narrative. The protagonist *is* the customer. And it's not enough to know simply who the customer is; you need to know what problem you're fixing and why in order to offer the solution. Until he sorted out these issues, Anuj had a technology but not a customer or a product.

At some point, the innovator must identify a customer need that the technology helps them solve. The combination of all those elements—customer, need, problem, solution—is required to transform a technology into a product. Finding a business model and way to go to market is what transforms your product into a business.

The good news for Anuj was that he already had a hypothesis about who the customer was and where to find them. He speculated that suburban commuting couples with only one car would value such a service. He thought they'd save money with a subscription-based alternative to Uber or public transportation for the partner who didn't get to use the car. Anuj wanted to trial the service in Sacramento, California. "Great!" I encouraged him. "You know the customer you'd like to target, you know where she lives, and now all you have to do is go talk to her."

Anuj did speak with customers, and to his surprise, he identified an entirely different problem to solve. He discovered that the most significant pain point for one-car families in these communities was grocery shopping. Customers were not satisfied with the costs and process of scheduling deliveries from multiple stores. Anuj and his team decided they'd use their technology to solve that problem. They explored building a solution where a consumer could create a shopping cart across multiple stores in one area, and Go360io would do pickup and a single delivery for all of them. In discovering the customer's real story, Anuj redirected his entire product strategy.

After pursuing this direction for a while, the team ultimately decided that a consumer business was not in their wheelhouse. They decided to pivot back to a business-to-business solution and leverage the most compelling technology they'd developed early on by creating powerful AI cameras for autonomous vehicles. Go360io morphed into Hyperspec AI cameras, which is selling their tech into the autonomous car industry. The point of this meandering innovation tale is that the customer will tell you whether your narrative is on point. If your product story is not resonating with your customer, you need to change it. Story is strategy, and if the story isn't working, the strategy must change.

The Innovation Narrative Storyboard Meets the Pitch Deck

The product story provides the foundation for your pitch deck. Develop an outline with about a dozen points in it. If it's a visual presentation, start with twelve slides. You can always add to this basic framework, but in the world of product pitches, less is usually more. Once you've got your presentation, you should be able to take someone through the logic and flow of your story without any visual aids. You need to know your story so well that you can leave the computer in your backpack and walk someone through the entire pitch. Many audiences prefer that you succinctly talk about your innovation without a fancy slide deck. There's a reason they call it an elevator pitch.

The storyboard is at the core of your pitch because your audience won't be interested in the other stuff if you don't establish a core product story first. As a listener, I'm not interested in your revenue model, market size, or any other business considerations until

I believe that you've identified a customer with a real problem that you've figured out how to solve. Once you have established those essential elements in the innovation narrative, then and only then do I want to hear about how you will turn it into a thriving business.

The first half-dozen or so slides are about the product narrative. Feel free to combine some of these elements into a single slide, but be sure to include the full product story. These points include the following:

1. **Customer**

2. **Insights**

3. **Problem statement**

4. **Value proposition**

5. **Product description and demo**

6. **Competitive advantage**

The above six points have been described in detail so far in the book. Now it's time to add the points that illustrate how you can turn it into a business.

7. **Traction:** Is anyone using this product yet, or do you have research from test users? Are they happy? Are there any paying customers? How has traction grown over time?

8. **Business model:** How are you going to make money? Is the end user going to pay for the product, or are you making money in another way? Do you expect any new

revenue streams as the business grows? What is the customer willing to pay?

9. **Go-to-market:** What is the market size? How does this break out by total available market (TAM), serviceable available market (SAM), and serviceable obtainable market (SOM)? How are you going to obtain customers? Is this a direct-to-consumer business? Will you need a retail channel? Will this require a sales force? Do you envision distribution partners?

10. **Team:** Who are you, and why are you uniquely suited to solve this problem and build this business? What have you done before this that is relevant to this product or business? Who else is on your team? Do you have advisers with experience in this industry or type of company?

11. **Ask:** What do you need? Funding? Strategic partners? If you require funding, what are you going to use it for?

That's eleven things to address. I start with one more. **The title slide**: What is your vision for this innovation?

The title slide displays the name of your company or product and includes below it either the value proposition or a product descriptor. This is where you provide your vision for how the world is going to be a better place with your product in it. It signals to your audience, "Hang in there while I build this product story." It will be worth it to the audience to let the story unfold. Once you've done so, you'll have more freedom to introduce your protagonist and dive into a compelling product story.

Take Strava. *Strava* means "strive" in Swedish. It is an app that enables athletes to track their athletic performance and share it with their community. It's clear, however, from their mission statement that they had a far bigger vision than simply to help people document their bike rides and neighborhood runs. Strava's mission statement is "to build the most engaged community of athletes in the world." This is the type of bold statement that founders typically use to open their presentations.

As a happy Strava user, I can say that there's no question they're realizing that vision. Strava lets me connect with other cyclists in my community and around the world to share our passion for zipping around on two wheels. And I'm not alone. Strava has over eighty-five million users, and they're reportedly growing over one million new users every month.

Should You Tell a Different Story Depending on the Audience?

The short answer is no. Yes, you must consider your audience when telling a story, but don't let that sidetrack you from building a core narrative for your innovation. You have to start with *one* baseline story for your product.

Once that's completed, you can tailor and evolve your presentation as necessary for different meetings with different audiences. A finance person will want to know more about your three-year financial plan. An engineer might want to drill down on the technology platform you plan to use to build the product. An investor might want to understand if your IP is protected and how you plan to go to market. But everyone needs to understand the core product story, and that's where you start. You need to answer these questions: Who's the customer, what do they want, and how are you going to deliver it in a differentiated way?

What Happens When There Is No Story?

There are some harsh lessons for product teams that never discover their narrative. Good technology alone will not win the day if it doesn't provide utility for someone. I'm sure you've heard the expression "That sounds like a technology looking for a problem to solve." The way to discover the value is to look for the right narrative—that is to say, who is going to benefit from your technology, what do they need, and how are you going to help them? Once you've discovered that narrative, you're on your way. If, on the other hand, you never figure out the narrative, you'll probably end up like one unfortunate product that didn't make it—Google Wave.

In May 2009, Google VP of Engineering, Vic Gundotra, unveiled a product at the Google I/O conference that he called "unbelievable and magical." A few months later, it was made available through private invitation to thousands of users. If you got one of those invitations back in the day, you had one of the most prized emails in Silicon Valley. The buzz was off the charts. And within little over a year, the product was off the market. Dead.

Failure is part of innovation, and Google has had enough groundbreaking successes to make up for a lifetime of missteps. But the story of Google Wave is informative. The product was described as a "hosted conversation that anyone can contribute to." It was a new communications tool, designed to outperform email, that was part chat, part wiki, part file sharing. The problem is that Google launched a technology, but they never figured out the rest of the story. What type of customer would use Google Wave? What were the issues with which the customer was struggling? What specific problem would it solve? What was the value proposition? Google never nailed down the answers to those questions at launch. In short, there was no narrative. Wave never got traction, and it died.

Fast-forward to today. A company called Slack has created a product that is highly reminiscent of Google Wave. The difference is that Slack *has* a story. The founder, Stewart Butterfield, had a specific customer in mind (business teams) and identified a big problem: They were using too many disconnected communications platforms. Butterfield created Slack to let them do all their messaging and file sharing in one place. I'd say it's worked out for Slack. Slack went public in 2019 with a valuation of nearly $20B.

>>>→

Act 2

How to Tell a Compelling Story

4

Use Your Brain.
Tell a Story.

arry Tesler was a scientist working at the famed Xerox PARC in 1979 when he led the most significant tech tour in the history of Silicon Valley. In some parallel universe, this tour didn't happen, and you never heard of an iPhone. But in *this* universe, Larry Tesler shared Xerox technology with the founder of a three-year-old computer company. The founder's name was Steve Jobs.

What Steve saw that day changed the course of his fledgling company. He envisioned a story that Xerox management did not. Steve saw a world where everyday people would access personal computing power through affordable and simple-to-use devices. The protagonist in Steve's story was not a computer programmer but a regular person. Simple tasks like using a computer to do word processing had not been possible for everyday people. But this new story emerged for Steve as he took the tour. The technology he saw at Xerox would make the impossible possible. If he could integrate this tech into his personal computers, he could solve the character's problem in his story. Steve got behind that narrative and became a master at telling the story. Xerox missed out.

So far, we've focused on making sure we have that strong story in place. The innovation storyboard is a tool, like an architect's blueprint, to assess the core elements of the story and ensure that we have something worth creating. With the blueprint down, we can shift our focus to *telling* a great story. If we don't tell a great story, our idea literally can be lost in an organization. That's exactly what happened at Xerox in the late 1970s.

Larry Tesler and I became colleagues at Yahoo! twenty-five years later, but I didn't realize at the time that he was the guy who gave Steve Jobs the view into the future that launched Apple as we know it. Steve had cut a deal with Xerox's venture arm to let him see the company's technology in exchange for the opportunity to buy one hundred thousand shares in Apple stock. According to Walter Isaacson's fantastic biography of Jobs,[5] the Xerox PARC staff was

---

5   Walter Isaacson, *Steve Jobs* (Simon & Schuster, 2011), p. 97.

reluctant to show him much at first. But Steve knew they were holding back, and angrily called the venture folks and demanded to see more. They agreed. What Larry then revealed to Steve literally changed the world of computing.

Larry showed Steve everything, including Xerox's creation of a graphical user interface (GUI or gooey for short), the desktop metaphor, and the mouse. The gooey was a game changer because Xerox found a way to create a bitmap that allowed for graphics—not just lines of code. Steve screamed, "You're sitting on a goldmine. I can't believe Xerox isn't taking advantage of this."

Some have argued that the timeline was different from Isaacson's narrative and that other Apple employees had seen these technologies even before Steve. But what is inarguable is that Xerox never fully commercialized the technology. Xerox PARC was a tremendous research operation that made important discoveries. But Xerox wasn't only a research operation; they also made products. Somehow, though, the idea of building and marketing a personal computer based on these technologies never gained traction within the company. Either they never understood the story or couldn't find a compelling way to tell it—or both. Steve, however, ran with the inspiration and introduced these innovations in the Lisa and the Macintosh. The rest is history. Xerox received a modest financial benefit from their investment. But Apple became Apple.

How does this happen? Why did it take another company to get these technologies out of the lab and into a product? How do great ideas get lost in an organization? Your concept is like a salmon swimming upstream. There are too many enemies for a good idea to survive on its own. Short attention spans, competing ideas, and risk aversion typically thwart innovation.

So how does the innovator *break through all this noise*? Storytelling. Successful innovations require passionate advocates who can tell a great story. An inspired storyteller grabs the audience's attention and gets them excited about a new idea.

The Brain Science Behind Storytelling

At first blush, cynics believe that storytelling is a soft skill, but neuroscience is behind the power of stories. It turns out that our species is wired for story, which is also the title of Lisa Cron's great book about storytelling. And because it's in our DNA, it is a powerful tool in the hands of an innovator. But let's start with the science.

Cron's book catalogs recent brain studies by neuroscientists and psychologists that explore how a brain processes stories. She describes how fundamentally different the brain behaves when consuming stories as opposed to straight facts and information. For most of the life of our species, we only *had* stories to share what we had learned. We told stories to help future generations understand how to navigate a scary world. And our brains became good at it.

In his seminal book, *Sapiens*, Yuval Noah Harari argues that our species enjoyed a cognitive revolution between seventy thousand and thirty thousand years ago, enabling us to separate from every other animal.[6] Other animals could communicate, but they

---

6   Yuval Noah Harari, *Sapiens* (Harper, 2015), Chapter 2.

could not transfer large amounts of information about their world. We could. Stories helped us build better tools and become more skilled hunters. They taught us how to behave. Through powerful narratives we shared information more broadly so that we could organize larger groups. We could even paint a picture of what a future world could look like. Those stories inspired communities, and ultimately civilizations, to bring that vision to fruition.

When we listen to a story, we effectively put ourselves in the shoes of the protagonist. We ask, "How would I react in this situation?" The neuroscientist Marco Iacoboni describes how our mirror neurons are activated when this happens.[7] They allow us to feel what others experience as if we were in the story ourselves. How else can you explain the fact that some of us cry at movies? (*Toy Story 3* was a killer for me.)

A study by researcher Jeffrey M. Zacks and several colleagues describes how MRI scans of the brain support this phenomenon. They report that the brain's areas that light up when you are reading about an experience are the same as those that light up when you *have* that experience yourself.[8]

Let's try this out.

In 2019, my wife, Carla, and I took our first trip to India. India is an assault on the senses. On a drive from Agra to Jaipur in the north, we passed food stands offering fresh-made rotis, spices, and roasted

---

7   Marco Iacoboni, interviewed by Jonah Lehrer, "The Mirror Neuron Revolution: Explaining What Makes Humans Social," *Scientific American*, July 1, 2008.

8   Nicole K. Speer, Jeremy R. Reynolds, Khena M. Swallow, Jeffrey M. Zacks, "Reading Stories Activates Neural Representations of Visual and Motor Experiences–2009," SAGE Journals.

delicacies. We were "accompanied" side-by-side on the roadways by a variety of animals—camels, dogs, pigs, elephants, water buffalo, and mules. Women in brilliant saris the color of marigolds carried shimmering silver water jugs on their heads; cars honked incessantly and hurtled seemingly directly at us before swerving into another lane. There were numerous wedding processions with dozens of revelers dancing behind slow-rolling trucks with massive speakers blaring Indian pop music. As we experienced that sensory overload, the parts of our brains that process those senses lit up. The *exact* same parts of *your* brain just lit up as you read that passage. When a story taps into our senses (touch, feel, sound, smell), it activates the insula in a way that doesn't happen when straight facts are related.

In his book *The Storytelling Animal*, Jonathan Gottschall writes, "Fiction seems to be more effective at changing beliefs than writing that is specifically designed to persuade through argument and evidence." Gottschall cites studies by the psychologists Melanie Green and Tim Brock that argue that stories "radically alter the way information is processed." The more absorbed people are in a story, the more the story affects them. Gottschall concludes that when we hear factual arguments, we listen to them "with our dukes up. We are critical and skeptical. But when we are absorbed in a story, we drop our intellectual guard. We are moved emotionally, and this seems to leave us defenseless."[9]

Great stories pique our curiosity; we must know what's going to happen next. The most captivating stories begin with a conflict or

---

9   Jonathan Gottschall, *The Storytelling Animal* (Mariner Books, 2012), p. 151.

a series of conflicts that the protagonist must overcome. Again, this all comes down to survival. If we know how others have handled certain situations, we'll be better prepared to handle them in our own lives. Stories were passed along to help our families and communities survive. It's in our DNA.

To be successful as an innovator, you must convey to your audience what your customer is going through at a visceral level. So when you're in front of an audience, put their entire brain to work and tell a story!

Michelle Crosby, the founder of Wevorce, tells a riveting story. She recounts the awful experience she went through as a child of divorce to help portray the characters in her product story and the problems they face. At the age of nine, Michelle's parents were unable to decide on custody, so a judge asked her, "Which parent would you like to live with?" What a heart-wrenching thing to put a kid through! When Michelle tells her origin story on camera, you see the pain of this moment etched on her face. She says, and her voice cracks a little, "When you're nine, you want to live with both."

Michelle created Wevorce to help couples through this extraordinarily challenging time and make the process of divorce more civil. Her story keeps her team focused on this problem and how to solve it; it's also instrumental in helping her gain a following. She was invited to join Y Combinator, an elite startup accelerator, and has raised over $5M to grow her business. Never underestimate the power of a compelling story. It's pure science.

How to Persuade

The storyteller's objective is to persuade. To persuade, she must ensure that her story is memorable, compelling, and clear. She uses three primary strategies to influence her audience:

1. Find the emotional hook.

2. Convey the logic in the story.

3. Make the story understandable.

Good storytellers deploy a myriad of approaches to achieve each of these three strategies. In the following chapters, I'll share a series of tactics to support each of them.

5

Strategy #1: Find the Emotional Hook

If your audience doesn't remember your pitch, it doesn't matter how compelling your product is. One of the best ways to ensure your audience remembers your story is to make them *feel something*.

Let's go back to the brain science behind the power of story. In his book *Brain Rules*, John Medina, the developmental molecular biologist, writes, "When the brain detects an emotionally charged event, the amygdala releases dopamine into the system. Because dopamine greatly aids memory and information processing, you could say it creates a Post-it note that reads, 'Remember this.'" Think about the last good book you read, the last movie you saw, or even the last video ad you tried to ignore. The one that touched you stayed with you. During the latest Academy Awards broadcast, Google aired a commercial featuring a Google employee named Tony who was a CODA, which stands for Child of a Deaf Adult. The ad features several Google products (search, messaging, and closed captioning on Google Meet), and it stays with you, because it tells a story. We see Tony's parents, who are both Deaf, getting married; we watch Tony grow up, translate for his parents, and then have a family of his own. In the final scene that took place during the isolation of the pandemic, Tony's parents share a moment with their first grandchild over Google Meet. Several pundits on social media noted that this ninety-second story was better than a lot of the movies being lauded during the show. Once you see this ad, it's hard to forget it, because of the way it makes you feel. And you'll feel good about the company that told the story.

The cognitive psychologist Jerome Bruner famously reported from his work that information is up to twenty-two times more memorable when delivered in narrative form. He once asked the rhetorical question, "Why are we so intellectually dismissive toward narrative?" He went on to wonder, "Why are we inclined to treat it as a rather trashy, entertaining way of thinking about . . . what we do with our minds?"[10]

---

10   John Crace, "Jerome Bruner: the Lesson of Story," *The Guardian*, March 27, 2007, referencing Bruner's lecture at Oxford University at a ceremony naming a building in his honor.

In my experience, people who consider themselves smart don't want to acknowledge that they can be moved to action by emotion. It's why we overload our presentations with facts and information and are reluctant to tell stories. We think it's below us. But when we think that way, all we are doing is showing our ignorance about the way our brain works. The fact is that emotion and memory are as connected as Hansel and Gretel, Bonnie and Clyde, and Ren and Stimpy. If we consciously choose not to tap into emotion when talking about our ideas, it's just bad business.

Following are some ways to make that emotional connection that provides a direct link to memory.

Get Personal

A personal story is a storyteller's secret weapon. A funny thing happens when we tell a personal story. We become more animated. Our eyes sparkle. We might even get more emotional, as Matt Cooper did in the story in chapter one. If we're talking about a problem, it feels more palpable and real to us. And guess what—it has the same effect on the audience. Your audience is more likely to lean forward and want to know what happens in the story, because it's a genuine story about your experience. That's exactly what happened to Surbhi Sarna.

A Scare Leads to a Search for a Cure

Imagine that you were the parent of a thirteen-year-old girl with cysts detected in her ovaries. Imagine that they might be cancerous.

And imagine that the doctors were unable to determine the nature of the cysts without dangerous invasive surgery.

Now imagine that you were the young girl. Surbhi Sarna was that girl. Thankfully, Surbhi survived this experience, and it inspired her to pursue a career addressing women's health issues. Ultimately, she chose to focus on this very issue—early ovarian cancer detection—and to start a company called nVision Medical that offered a solution. To date, clinicians have been unable to perform a biopsy or direct visualization of the fallopian tubes, because the tubes are 1 mm in diameter and tortuous. Surbhi's company is developing better ways to view and collect cells from a woman's fallopian tubes.

Like many entrepreneurs, Surbhi struggled to get her venture off the ground. One day, Surbhi was meeting with Tim Draper, one of Silicon Valley's top venture capitalists. Until that moment, Surbhi had never shared the story of her own frightening ovarian cancer scare. She thought it was too personal and inappropriate in a business context. But for whatever reason, it came out in her conversation with Draper. He was shocked. He told Surbhi that she *had* to tell this story whenever she talked about her young company because it conveyed her knowledge of the problem and, most importantly, demonstrated her unwavering commitment to solving it. In conferences, Surbhi began talking about how she changed from being a "patient to an impatient entrepreneur." A photo of her mother on the screen behind her, she says with a catch in her voice, "I wanted to solve this problem so others didn't have to suffer what my mother and I suffered."

By telling this story to prospective investors and executing brilliantly, Surbhi raised over $4M for her company nearly overnight. She built the business and sold it to Boston Scientific for $150M and the potential to reach $275M if the company clears regulatory hurdles in the coming years. That's the power of a personal story.

Bring the Customer into the Room

At the 2015 State of the Union address, President Obama wanted to convey how government-funded initiatives helped the middle class emerge from the financial crisis of 2007–08. But rather than just list a bunch of programs, he told the story of Rebekah and Ben Erler of Minneapolis. Rebekah was in the House Chamber sitting between the First Lady and Jill Biden as the president spoke.

The president recounted that Rebekah and Ben Erler led a charmed life. They were newlyweds; had a son, Henry; and were "young and in love in America . . . and it doesn't get much better than that."[11] But then 2007 came along. Ben lost his construction job during the financial crisis, and things looked dark for the family. The president then talked about how the story turned. And it turned in a place where government support for the middle class met individual initiative.

Rebekah took out student loans and enrolled at a community college to be retrained. She found a job in her new field and kept the family going until the economy recovered, and Ben was able to

---

11   Barack Obama, "State of the Union Address," January 20, 2015.

get rehired in construction. The president noted that they worked, sacrificed, and retooled, and then he shared what Rebekah wrote to him: "We are a strong, tight-knit family," she said, "that's made it through some very hard times." He repeated it: "We are a strong, tight-knit family that's made it through some very hard times." The president wanted to make the point that Americans needed to pivot (retool), and the federal government had provided the student loans that made Rebekah's new training possible. This was the most memorable moment of the entire address because he brought the customer into the room. He struck a chord. He brought the customer to life.

When you are fighting to defend your idea, your most powerful ally is the customer. Bring them into the room (at least figuratively) and make their pain as real as possible. In intrapreneurial settings, I've seen this play out over and over again. Executives often become inured to reams of data about unhappy customers. However, if you tell them about a specific customer named, say, Sam who had a miserable experience, watch what happens. Every time you see the executive after that, they're likely to ask, "What are we doing for Sam? Are we solving Sam's problem? Is Sam happy now?"

Grab Your Audience from the Jump

Start your presentation with a bang. There's a reason why every James Bond film starts with an elaborate chase scene. In *Spectre*, for example, Bond runs along a rooftop, jumps onto a flying helicopter, and then wrestles an assailant while hanging from the copter's landing skids high above a pulsating Día de los Muertos parade in Mexico City. It is no accident that this and so many other movies open with an incredibly dramatic scene.

Storytellers know that job one is to grab the audience's attention. Some storytellers call this *vertical takeoff*. (Yes, there is a reason I chose to feature the helicopter scene from all the Bond movies!) And there's science behind it. When we see or hear something dramatic, it activates a hormone called cortisol, the stress gland. This makes us focus. Have you ever driven down the freeway, listening to music, chatting with a friend, and all of a sudden the car in front of you slams on the breaks? You instantly turn all your attention to braking safely. That's cortisol at work. Likewise, once the audience is locked in, focused, and leaning forward, you've got them.

Start your presentation by telling a good story, showing a striking visual or video, sharing a shocking statistic, or asking a provocative question. Whatever you do, don't start with an agenda or an apology for being late! Grab their attention! Like this . . .

A Silent Problem

"I was born in a Deaf family." Thibault Duchemin, a young French entrepreneur, stepped to the front of the room at his SkyDeck Demo Day and immediately grabbed his audience with that simple declarative statement. "My parents are Deaf. My sister is Deaf. I know how painful it is to understand group conversations when you can't hear well. You are so focused on reading the lips of the person in front of you when somebody else starts speaking. You turn your head, and you miss the first words. But because you miss those words, you miss the whole conversation. But that wasn't only my family. There are four hundred million people who suffer from disabling hearing loss."

The audience was instantly drawn into Thibault's personal story and understood the problem and its scale. In less than thirty seconds, he grabbed our attention ("I was born in a Deaf family"), vividly helped us grasp a problem we never thought about ("following group conversations when you can't hear well"), and conveyed that a *lot* of people share this problem ("four hundred million people"). Thibault added that the only surefire way to keep up was to hire someone to document a conversation in real time (through live captioning) at $120/hour. Would you bring a captioner to a dinner party at that rate?

The audience was hooked and edged up in their seats to hear how he was going to solve the problem.

Thibault and a team led by cofounder Skinner Cheng, who cannot hear, realized the best way to create a universal solution would be to tap the ubiquity of smartphones. They built the app Ava (www.ava.me), which transcribes conversations in real time and shows the user who said what. They are making it possible for Deaf people to communicate in group conversations easily in work or social situations. Ava has won numerous startup competitions, raised over $6M, and launched its app to begin serving this community. During the COVID-19 pandemic, Ava was being used in audiology clinics to help patients who were unable to either read the lips or hear the muffled voices of their care providers through masks.

Give Your Idea a Strong Handle

Good ideas benefit from strong handles. A thoughtful name helps us create a space in our mind to house new ideas. It has the effect of creating a "cubbyhole" that we can fill with information about a concept. It helps us retain and retrieve the notions associated with that innovation.

Two of the most significant social movements of the last decade—Black Lives Matter and #MeToo—strongly support this. These social justice movements were a product of shared frustration and anger among a large group of disenfranchised people. They both used social media to rapidly fuel the passion of others who shared a similar enthusiasm for these issues. They shared stories of people who suffered terribly at the hands of racism in the case of BLM or powerful sexual predators (predominantly men) in the case of #MeToo. But both of these initiatives also benefited greatly from having a memorable handle.

Black Lives Matter was the creation of Alicia Garza, Patrisse Cullors, and Opal Tometi in 2013 after the acquittal of Trayvon Martin's murderer, George Zimmerman. Alicia, Patrisse, and Opal wanted to convey the notion that throughout the history of the United States, Black lives *have not* always mattered. White people have created policies and institutions for hundreds of years— from slavery to reconstruction to the Jim Crow era to present-day instances of police brutality—that have repeatedly demonstrated that Black lives are not treated equally. Thus, the call for change.

#MeToo was created in 2006 by Tarana Burke to support victims of sexual harassment and assault. In 1997, Tarana was listening to a thirteen-year-old girl recount an experience of sexual abuse. Tarana was unable to say what she wanted to say to that little girl: "Me too." A decade later she created a nonprofit organization to help these victims and coined the phrase "me too" to convey that so many people have suffered from similar acts of violence. After Harvey Weinstein was accused of sexual harassment, assault, and rape in 2017, the actress Alyssa Milano popularized "me too" by calling on other women who suffered similarly to tell their stories under the banner of #MeToo.

When people talk about these movements today, they have an easy way to ground the conversation. Just mentioning "Black Lives Matter" or "#MeToo" brings to mind a world of associations and emotion. They are strong handles that empower activists to build followers, make demands, and strive for social change.

New ideas for businesses also benefit from a good name; just ask JetBlue. JetBlue's problem started on a snowy Valentine's Day in 2007. Numerous JetBlue planes remained stranded on New York City runways for up to nine hours. Because of several poor procedures, the passengers were stuck on the planes with nothing to eat. The aircrafts never returned to their gates. They just sat there. And this happened on the most romantic day of the year when most travelers just wanted to get home to their loved ones. In the following days, passengers shared their war stories, and it became a PR nightmare. The airline had always touted the JetBlue Experience as the best experience in the sky. That was a hard claim to maintain after their Valentine's Day nightmare.

The CEO was horrified and quickly invested $30M in new

procedures to improve operations during bad weather. JetBlue also introduced a new idea. They decided that their customers should have a certain set of rights that the airline should live up to. They decided that if they didn't meet this basic level of service, they would compensate their customers. They called the new program the JetBlue Bill of Rights.

The right name for a product or program can be instrumental in making an innovation stick with customers. JetBlue's initiative made an impression on its customers because the program name instantly conveyed that the customer would have some power. This was a novel idea for the airline and was instrumental in helping passengers understand that they would have avenues for redress if the airline failed them.

Share an Authentic Origin Story

What started as a quick visit home to New York from Harvard Business School turned into an epiphany for Jennifer Hyman—an epiphany that led to a business now valued at hundreds of millions of dollars. Jenn was in her sister Becky's room hanging out when Becky began fretting about an upcoming wedding she'd be attending. She was staring at her closet full of clothes, but as far as Becky was concerned, she had absolutely nothing to wear. To make matters worse, she had recently purchased a gorgeous dress for $2,000—which was more than her rent—but she'd already worn it, and there were pictures of her in it. She felt she couldn't *possibly* wear it to the next event. That's when the light bulb went on for Jenn.

Becky wanted to look great for the wedding, so that meant she wanted a fabulous dress. But Becky was at the age where she'd be going to *lots* of weddings—often with the same group of friends—and she *couldn't* wear the same dress more than once. Guys can get away with wearing the same suit or tux, but with women it's a different story. Becky couldn't afford to buy a different designer dress for each wedding, and she felt stuck. That's where Jenn's inspiration happened. What if you could *rent* a unique, fantastic dress for every big event you attended? That would solve Becky's problem!

She and her classmate Jennifer Fleiss immediately kicked the idea around, and Rent the Runway was born. They cold-emailed Diane von Furstenberg to pitch the idea because the designers would have to embrace the concept as well. Amazingly, she responded and invited them to a meeting the next day. Diane von Furstenberg didn't buy into the idea immediately, but she gave them some encouragement.

The two Jennifers kept developing their idea and created a service where women can rent a different high-end designer dress (think Herve Leger or Proenza) for any special event. Rent the Runway lets people like Becky pick out a dress online and then receive a couple of different sizes in the mail so one is sure to fit. The Jennifers raised over $100M to build their business.

We don't always have an origin story worth sharing. That's OK. In fact, it often takes too long to fold it into a short pitch presentation anyway. But in some instances, sharing an origin story is the perfect way to engage your audience and help them understand your overall innovation narrative. Women, in particular, relate to this story. The storyteller's job is to make sure that *anyone* in her audience can empathize with the character in the story, even if it's not in their own life experience. Rent the Runway's website still features this story today nearly a dozen years after it happened. It remains relevant and compelling to RTR customers.

The origin story paints a picture that draws people in and illustrates an essential aspect of your story. Becky's "closet full of clothes and nothing to wear" moment did two things: (1) It conveyed the actual origin story of Rent the Runway (people love origin stories), and (2) it vividly illustrated the core insight behind this innovation.

When telling your origin story, be sure to paint a picture and name names. The more specifics you share about the people and events in a story, the more memorable it will be.

Tell a Story That Conveys Your Purpose

In today's America, Neil deGrasse Tyson may be the most famous astrophysicist this side of Galileo. But he almost didn't become one. He tells a wonderful story about how he initially found his purpose. The purpose story is a hugely compelling strategy for anyone trying to convey why they've sacrificed so much of their life to do what they do.

Neil was in graduate school at Columbia University, working in the lab when the phone rang. It was a day that changed his life. The call came at a time when Tyson was rethinking his life's work. He had a fascination for the universe and loved his course of study, but a friend had been nagging him to do something more useful. His friend, who is Black and worked in poor communities, had said to Neil, who is also Black, "Astrophysics? The Black community cannot afford the luxury of someone with your intellect to spend it on that subject." Tyson explains, "I was devastated by that comment." It remained "an albatross around my neck" and made him doubt what he had chosen to do with his life.[12]

OK, now the phone call. On the other end was someone from the local Fox News affiliate. The weatherman had read on the news wire that there was an explosion on the sun—a blast of plasma. He wanted to better understand what that meant for citizens of Earth. Tyson described what happened with the "charged particles from the Sun" and how it would create the northern lights. The station asked, "So Earth is OK?" And Tyson said, "The Earth is fine." "Great," the TV folks said. "Can you say that on the air?"

"I go home. Call *everybody*!" Tyson recalls. "I'm gonna be on TV!" At the end of the broadcast, Tyson says, "I had an epiphany. A revelation. It was 1989. I had never before in my life . . . seen an interview with a Black person on TV that had nothing to do with being Black. I'm talking about experts . . . the guy didn't ask me, 'Well, how do *Black* people feel about this plasma coming from the sun. How does *your* community feel about this? Will it harm *your* skin the way it will harm ours?' That was *not* the conversation! I was telling [him] whether Earth would survive."

Tyson realized he could change the perceptions of those who thought Black folks couldn't be intellectuals. "Smart is saved for

---

12   Dr. Neil DeGrasse Tyson, interviewed by Dr. Thomas Cech, *Adventures of an Urban Astrophysicist*, Howard Hughes Medical Institute Program, 2008.

scientists," he says. And Neil wanted people to see a Black person in that role. He realized that astrophysics had to remain his calling. He says, "That would have a greater force on society than anything else I could imagine. It's not that the Black community can't afford me to do astrophysics; they can't afford to have me *not* do astrophysics."

Everyone has a story. The best personal stories include some extraordinary obstacles to overcome. I heard one of those stories at a program for global environmental leaders where I teach.

Binta Iliyasu was one of the environmental leaders who attended the Beahrs Environmental Leadership Program at UC Berkeley. Binta was born in Northern Nigeria. She grew up in a village where girls were expected to work in the home and not get an education. A teacher recognized twelve-year-old Binta's intellect and gave her an unusual opportunity to take an entrance exam to continue her schooling. This was not common for young girls. Some older women in her village spoke to Binta and pleaded with her to answer the exam questions incorrectly so she wouldn't advance any further. They told her this was not the proper path for a young girl.

Binta didn't listen. She took the test and proceeded to the next level. Thankfully, her parents supported her. When she reached her twenties and was old enough to marry, she faced another challenge. Only one man was willing to back Binta's continued studies. So Binta married him and continued her education.

As Binta tells this story before a crowd of environmental donors, she proudly says, "Today I stand before you as a biochemist . . . the best in my class. The first female in my community of hundreds of households . . . a principal research officer with the Nigerian Office of Trypanosomiasis Research." She's now working to improve the lives of rural sub-Saharan, small-holder farming communities. Binta came to this program in the US to continue a lifelong quest to overcome every obstacle to continue her learning so she could make a difference in the world. In telling the story, she took her audience with her to her small village in sub-Saharan Africa, where we watched the beginning of a stubborn little girl's journey to become an extraordinary environmental leader.

Every story in this chapter shares something in common. They're all memorable. Whether it's Surbhi's experience overcoming an ovarian cancer scare with her mother by her side, Thibault's story of growing up as the only hearing person in his family, Jennifer's story about her sister's wardrobe dilemma, or Binta's remarkable journey from her village to becoming a biochemist improving the lives of farmers, they all resonate with us on an emotional level. Each story was different in how it made us feel. One story might have been sad, another funny, another moving or perhaps surprising. Regardless of how they made us feel, however, they made us feel *some*thing. Because we felt something, we're going to remember what we heard. If the storyteller is able to find the emotional hook, they've accomplished their number-one goal. They've told a memorable story.

6

Strategy #2: Make the Story Logical

There is a logic to the structure of stories. We get to know a character, learn about their motivations, discover what's keeping them from getting where they want to go, and then learn (in a happy story) how and why they got what they wanted. In an innovation story, we also look for this parallel structure. The storyteller has to set up the customer issues up front and then resolve them with the product at the back end. There's a simple logic to a good innovation story. There are many ways to get your audience nodding and thinking, *Oh, this makes sense.* To make your story compelling, always be sure to connect the dots. Set up the story and pay it off. Your narrative must make sense.

Romance the Problem

The setup to a good story usually starts with the storyteller portraying a great problem to overcome. In that way, it's satisfying (and logical) to the listener when the protagonist finally overcomes it. One of the most celebrated touchstones in recent American culture is a musical about America's first secretary of the treasury. To make Alexander Hamilton's life compelling, the playwright Lin-Manuel Miranda introduced the problem of the play's hero overcoming his impoverished immigrant beginnings right at the top of the play. The first lyrics in the song are literally a litany of the challenges he has to overcome:

"How does a bastard, orphan, son of a whore

And a Scotsman, dropped in the middle of a forgotten spot

In the Caribbean by Providence impoverished

In squalor, grow up to be a hero and a scholar?"

Miranda purposefully detailed the many problems Hamilton faced as a young man coming of age. The ability to romance the problem is an invaluable arrow in the storyteller's quiver. The bigger the conflict the character has to overcome, the more satisfying the ending. Writers refer to this as raising the stakes. It's not enough to identify that something stands in the way of our protagonist. Your audience needs to believe that the consequences of not overcoming the obstacle are massive. When introducing the challenge your customer faces, lean into the problem. If I don't think it's that big a deal, why should I care about hearing what you've created to solve it?

One approach is to introduce a compelling statistic that dramatically illustrates the scale of the problem. Don't overburden your audience with numbers; rather, find a single data point that demonstrates the magnitude of the issue. Alternatively, create a striking visual that illustrates the problem or introduce a powerful anecdote. Here's an example.

The Potentially Fatal Heartbeat

Connor Landgraf is a boyish twentysomething entrepreneur invited to speak to potential investors at DEMO Enterprise 2014. Connor began his talk by playing the audio of two heartbeats, which sound almost exactly the same. "Thump thump thump thump." Then the other one: "Thump thump thump thump." "Can you hear the difference?" Connor asked. "I don't know about you, but for me, it's really challenging."

One of the heartbeats is normal. The other is the sound of a split S-1, a congenital heart defect that can be potentially life threatening. If that's not scary enough, Connor said that four out of five new primary care physicians could not accurately diagnose heart conditions with an ordinary stethoscope, according to a study in the *AMA Journal*. This is clearly a *big* problem to solve. Connor has identified a life-threatening issue, he's provided a single data point that demonstrates the scale of the problem, and he's done it by tapping into one of our senses (sound). He has efficiently romanced the problem, and the audience is intrigued. They are hungry to hear how he is going to solve it.

Connor's startup, Eko Devices, created a solution to address this problem. It's a digital device that connects to an ordinary stethoscope. Using the Eko-enhanced stethoscope, doctors can record heart sounds and then map them using a smartphone app to over fifty thousand heart sounds in Eko's database. Doctors use this mechanism to accurately detect various heart conditions. More than four hundred hospitals and health providers now use this product.[13]

Komal Ahmad, like Connor, was another college student who set out to solve a big problem. She calls it the "world's dumbest problem." Komal coined the phrase while speaking on the floor of the United Nations.

I met Komal in 2012 when she dropped in during my office hours to discuss her nonprofit idea called Feeding Forward. She told me the story of stumbling across a homeless veteran named John on Telegraph Avenue across the street from the Berkeley campus. For some reason, he got her attention, and she bought him lunch. Over their meal, John explained that he hadn't received his veteran benefits in weeks, and as a result, he hadn't

---

13   Eko White Paper, *Guthrie Hospital System*, Eko Case Studies, ekohealth.com

eaten in three days. When Komal told this story years later at the UN, she said, "Imagine. Three whole days without food." This seemed so "dumb" to Komal because her campus dining hall was "wasting tons of food" right across the street. "I watched food being thrown away on one side of the street and people starving on the other side." But this problem was much bigger than what she experienced in Berkeley.

In her UN speech, Komal explained that 50 million people go to bed hungry every night, while 365 million pounds of perfectly good food gets tossed in the trash every single day in America. Komal often said, "Hunger isn't a scarcity problem; it's a logistics problem." Resolving the disparity between excess food and *access* to food became her life's mission. Komal gave her UN speech on the first day of Ramadan and while fasting she shared, "Despite my pangs of hunger, I know at sunset, I will have food to eat. Unfortunately, that's not the case for millions of others. The sun never sets on their hunger."

Komal used a personal narrative, a purposeful anecdote, and two powerful data points to romance the problem. Anyone listening to her story was desperate to hear how she was going to solve it. Komal eventually transformed her nonprofit Feeding Forward into a for-profit technology company called Copia—a marketplace that connects those with excess food with nonprofits and shelters that need it most. Komal has been named in Entrepreneur Magazine's "100 Powerful Women" list, made *Forbes* magazine's 30 under 30 list twice, and was honored with the prestigious Nelson Mandela Humanitarian Award.

Identify the Antagonist in Your Story

One foolproof strategy to romance the problem is identifying the enemy and making your product the hero. A recent VatorNews article ran with the headline "Every Unicorn Needs a Nemesis." A unicorn is a startup that has achieved a billion-dollar valuation. Take Uber. Their nemesis was the taxi industry. Airbnb had the hotel industry as its foil. If you identify an incumbent solution with all sorts of problems, then *your* solution can arrive like a superhero—or a superhero riding on a unicorn—to save the day.

With the creation of the 1984 TV commercial for the Macintosh, entitled "1984," Steve Jobs set the gold standard for dramatizing the antagonist in their story. At the time, IBM, of course, was the enemy. Comparing IBM—known then as Big Blue—to George Orwell's Big Brother was a stroke of genius. Later Steve demonized Microsoft in the equally famous Mac vs. PC campaign.

A more recent example is from the shaving company Harry's. They recently produced a funny video where the voiceover announcer says their mission is to take on "Big Razor" (Gillette). They list all the annoying things about Big Razor that Harry's addresses with their direct-to-consumer model. Harry's took this strategy straight to the bank. In seven years, they built Harry's into such a successful business that the *other* big shaving company (Schick) announced plans to buy them for $1.37B! Sadly for both parties, the FTC challenged the acquisition, and Schick ultimately dropped its bid.

But perhaps my favorite story of identifying the enemy is the story of an emerging fashion brand based in San Francisco started by one of my students. Shilpa Shah and her cofounder, Karla Gallardo, wanted to create a fashion business that honored the artisans who created beautiful women's accessories from all over the world. They named it Cuyana, which means "to love" in Quechua, the language of Indigenous people from western South America. Shilpa and Karla wanted their customers to love not only the products but also the people behind them. They wanted to share the stories of leather makers from Argentina, alpaca farmers from Peru, and silk craftspeople from Japan. As a child, Shilpa went to India with her parents to visit family, and they would regularly visit local tailors who made beautiful clothing. Karla had the same experience growing up in Colombia. They both loved the work of local artisans.

As their business plan came into focus, however, the cofounders saw another narrative emerging. They were trying to fill a gap in the market between high-end fashion and the fast-growing low-end players. Karla and Shilpa realized that there was a clear enemy in their story and decided to name it and take it on. That enemy was fast fashion.

Top fast fashion brands like Zara, Topshop, and H&M have become hugely popular. H&M, for example, is valued at tens of billions of dollars. Their customers flock to their stores because they can afford up-to-date fashion for prices that used to be out of reach. They just need to sacrifice quality. You might wear clothes from these brands for a season, but they won't last, and it's on to something else. Karla and Shilpa felt that women should not need to sacrifice quality for fashion that wouldn't look out of date.

They extended their accessories line to include blouses, dresses, and skirts that provide a classic, timeless quality. These were garments that working women could afford and that they could wear for several seasons. They were promoting *anti*–fast fashion. And their business started to grow.

After they created their tagline "Fewer, Better Things," business quickly accelerated. With it, they conveyed their story and implicitly slammed the fast fashion phenomenon, which was effectively "more, cheap things." Karla and Shilpa successfully raised tens of millions of dollars and opened seven retail shops across the country to supplement their core online business. Cuyana is reportedly worth $50–$100M today.

Answer the Question, Why Now?

The famed venture capital firm Sequoia Capital has a note on its guide to building a pitch deck that reads, "Nature hates a vacuum; why hasn't your solution been built before now?" People are naturally skeptical. They assume that if there was a problem that needed to be solved, someone would have solved it already. This is logical. To ensure that your story addresses this logic problem, it's often a good idea to answer the question, Why now? Timing is everything. Your innovation narrative will be more compelling if the solution is particularly timely. Convey that now is the perfect moment to address the problem that you've identified.

Starbutter AI had a strong "why now" when they pitched their AI-driven tool to recommend credit cards to their millennial audience. Advancements in AI and voice recognition combined with an app-hungry demographic created the perfect moment for Starbutter AI's recommendation engine.

But Starbutter AI wasn't the only new financial product for millennials with a strong "why now." A young fintech company called Rize made this a central part of its story.

"Hi, my name is Justin Howell, I'm the cofounder and CEO of Rize, and I'm here to talk about the eighty million millennials in this country who are collectively saving nothing. Not a dime. This is a problem." Howell is giving his demo-day pitch in his 500 Startups cohort in 2016. "If your son or daughter moves back home after college to save money on rent, they're never leaving!" Justin has delivered a wonderful vertical takeoff to kick his presentation into gear. But he's also simply conveyed his "why now."

When Justin gave his pitch, millennials were between the ages of twenty and thirty-five. Most had entered the job market and were in their early earning years. They came of age during the financial crisis of 2008 and were skeptical of traditional financial instruments. This is a group that was earning money but not saving any. They wanted simple, manageable financial solutions on their mobile devices. This combination presented the perfect storm for Rize. They built a mobile app that did a few things: (1) It made it easy for their customers to set targets for specific needs (e.g., renting an apartment, creating a rainy-day fund, or saving money for a trip); (2) it provided peer comparisons; and (3) it moved the money. Rize made it easy for its customers to save on average $300 per month. It eventually pivoted and became a B2B answer for banks looking for slick digital solutions for their youngest customers, but it still has a great "why now."

Make the Product the Hero

If you've effectively romanced the problem, then the payoff for your story comes when you make the product the hero to come save the day for your customer. Stories have a rhythm, and we've come to expect a certain pattern or logic to how a story is told. When the central through line of a story goes unresolved, we're disappointed, but when the plot points come together, we're satisfied because our expectations have been met. Likewise, in a well-structured innovation story, your audience will have a natural rooting interest for your solution to arrive on the scene, fix the burdensome issues, and sweep the customer off their feet.

Kent Frankovich is a robotics engineer and entrepreneur, but he's also a bit of a showman. In fact, he taught *me* a thing or two about storytelling. While riding his bike home from his Stanford robotics lab one night on a dark city street, Kent noticed that his self-described "dinky little" headlight barely lit up the road in front of him and did virtually nothing to make him visible, especially from the side. He did some research and discovered that 70 percent of bike accidents were the result of low side visibility. As a tinkerer, Kent started to play around with creative ways to affix lights to the wheels of his bike, and soon Revolights was born.

When I met Kent, he was looking for a little help in prepping his pitch to an angel investor group hosting a startup competition.

We worked on his story, which included featuring his epiphany and sharing bike accident statistics to romance the problem. But it wasn't until the competition, when Kent was full stride into his pitch, that he reminded *me* of an important storytelling lesson. Make the product the hero!

The excitement started after Kent turned the lights out. Kent's bike stood in the room, and once the room was pitch black, he turned on the Revolights and spun the wheels. The leading half of the front wheel lit up in brilliant white, and the trailing half of the rear wheel sparkled in fire-engine red. There was a gasp from the audience, oohs and aahs, and everyone applauded! Kent won the competition hands-down.

It was a great reminder that innovation is the thing. Always make the product the centerpiece of the show! While you can't always do a product demo, especially when you're at the early development stage of an idea, you have to find a way to make the product concept tangible and exciting to your audience. You have several options: do a live demo like Kent (or Connor Landgraf with the Eko Devices stethoscope); prepare a recorded demo or video; or present some key visual that illustrates the product or service and how it works. Don't expect your audience to imagine how this brand-new product functions; you have to bring it to life.

It's one thing to be moved by a story, but it's another challenge altogether to have it make sense. When you've finished telling your innovation story, you want your audience to be nodding and thinking, "Wow, that's a really good idea; what a smart way to solve that problem." A student of mine, who was working on an idea to transform the process of digitizing massive amounts of documents, demonstrated this beautifully. In describing the innovation, the student did a thorough job of romancing the problem. The student portrayed the drudgery of the job by creating an antagonist in the story—boredom. The adult women who worked in the massive Japanese factories where this work took place mindlessly repeated the same steps as they dismantled bound documents and fed them into scanners. The student then made the product the hero by describing a new method that (1) eliminated the most monotonous aspects of preparing and scanning the documents and (2) gamified the process of managing the scans to make it fun. Sensors and machine vision enabled by IOT (Internet of Things) powered this innovation and provided the "why now." By the end of the story, I was rooting for these workers to have more fun on the job, and I completely bought into the solution that would make that possible. It was logical, compelling, moving, and therefore a successful story.

Z

Strategy #3: Make Your Story Understandable

When my son was a teen, he played massively multiplayer online games and was a particular fan of World of Warcraft (WOW). He immersed himself in WOW. If he wasn't playing, he was reading blog posts and learning new strategies. He read the comment sections religiously, but there were certain long threads he never read. "tl;dr," he'd mutter.

I thought tl;dr must be code for some arcane gaming technique. But it was just another teen abbreviation I had yet to learn. tl;dr? It means "Too long. Didn't read."

Be Brief

tl;dr is the enemy of any good story. Cut out the excess! Telling a concise story is hard but worth the effort. Thanks to help from my editor, I rewrote the prior paragraph and cut it in half. Mark Twain once said, "I would have written you a short letter, but I didn't have the time." (It's easy to write page after page of a long letter.) It's much more challenging to find the true essence of your story. But that's your job. The key to making a story clear is to keep it short. Half of the art of telling an understandable story is deciding which parts to leave out!

Keep the Product Story Simple

In describing your product or service, try to adhere to the rule of three. Your audience will have a hard time understanding your story if you can't boil down the product's description to a few key points. Let's go back to Komal Ahmad's story about her company Copia for a proper illustration.

Komal's story about meeting John, a homeless and hungry veteran, launched her mission to solve the world's dumbest problem. To address this issue, Komal created a marketplace that provides an economic benefit to any institution with a lot of food waste.

Here's how Copia works in three simple points:

1. **Request:** Using the app, institutions seamlessly schedule a pickup of surplus food, which they pay Copia to retrieve.

2. **Recover:** A network of drivers safely recovers the food and redistributes it to local shelters and organizations in the community.

3. **Report:** Copia issues a detailed report that documents the value of the surplus food to allow institutions access to millions in tax deductions as well as social and environmental impact metrics.

In summarizing the solution, Copia employs the rule of three: (1) request, (2) recover, (3) report. Anyone hearing the story can retain the information. The listener can walk out of the room and easily convey to others what Copia does and how it works. With this simple story, Komal has received tens of thousands of requests from all over the world to expand her platform and services globally.

Eko Devices and Spark Microgrants also adhere to the rule of three.

Eko Devices, intelligent stethoscope:

1. **Capture it:** Digital stethoscope records patient's heartbeat.

2. **Analyze** it: AI algorithms identify potential for heart disease.

3. **Share it:** Mobile and web software allows for easy sharing for second opinions.

Spark Microgrants, local impact projects:

1. **Empower local decision-making:** Villagers determine which projects to fund.

2. **Crowd-source the funding:** Enable anyone, anywhere to fund projects.

3. **Local ownership of the project:** Communities build the facilities themselves.

Create an Analog

As a basketball-loving teen growing up in Massachusetts, imagine my surprise one summer day when I biked past my local playground and saw a Boston Celtic playing on my court. I freaked! It was Steve Kuberski, who was the sixth-best player on the team, but still a Celtic! I had to get into that game.

There was a problem, though. I wasn't wearing my high-top basketball sneakers. I turned around, raced back home, threw my high-tops in my backpack, and leapt back on my bike. I was so amped-up that I allowed the straps from my backpack to get caught up in my spokes. Awkward!!! It seemed to take forever to untangle the mess, but I managed to return in time to play a quick game with one of my heroes. It worked out in the end, but what I needed when I first rode past the park was immediate access to something that was elsewhere. I needed a magic pocket I could reach into and pull out whatever I needed.

The magic pocket is the very analog that founder Drew

Houston used when he launched his revolutionary file-sharing product Dropbox. Dropbox was a foreign concept at first, so he described it as a magic pocket for your digital files. In a short introductory video, the announcer said, "You've all been there; you get to where you're going, and you've left your wallet or phone at home. Don't you wish you had a magic pocket?" The video then explained that Dropbox was effectively a magic pocket for your files. Anywhere you go, you can access your digital files via Dropbox on any device. They had created a real-world magic pocket!

If the idea you are developing is a bit hard to grasp, an analog will often help your audience understand it. Analogs give listeners a clear frame of reference for new concepts. Going back to the story of the Rotimatic, the entrepreneur, Pronoti Nagarkar, was a big fan of the analog. She compared her Rotimatic to a rice cooker. I've told the Rotimatic story many times, and I always ask how many people know what a roti is. A few hands usually go up. But when I ask, "Who has heard of a rice cooker?" *everyone* raises their hand, and the light goes on. This simple analogy helps people instantly grasp how the device could become a standard appliance in Indian kitchens all over the world. A good analog is often the most memorable and effective part of an innovation story.

Put on a Show

If you want your story to be clear, approach your presentation as if you were staging a play or reading to a child. Make it interesting.

And what's the key to putting on a great show? Let's go with the rule of three: (1) rehearse, (2) engage, and (3) convey confidence.

1. **Rehearse.** Practice your presentation. Get feedback from friends. Make it better. Practice again. Part of the rehearsal process includes staging. Scope out the room you will be in. Test out your equipment, check the lighting and sound. Determine where to stand so you can best connect with your audience.

2. **Engage.** Watch your audience and carefully observe how they are responding, and react accordingly.

3. **Convey confidence.** Use positive body language and bring variety to your voice. Your posture and voice should convey, "I have great belief in this idea." Project your voice to all corners of the room and use inflection. Lift your voice in certain moments and lower it in others. Take your time so the presentation doesn't feel rushed. Your audience is not merely buying your idea; they are also "buying" you! Speak with conviction and let them know you're not going to stop until this innovation happens.

Remember, You're Giving a Performance!

With my students, I love watching a great scene from the TV series *Mad Men* that beautifully illustrates this approach. If you get a chance, find it on Vimeo by searching for "Mad Men Carousel."

In the scene, the main character, Don Draper, a 1960s ad guy, tries to persuade Kodak executives to call their new projector something other than "the wheel." He's also inspiring them to do something unheard of back then—use emotion to sell technology.

Draper starts the meeting by telling an anecdote about an old Greek copywriter he worked for named Teddy. Teddy said that the most powerful way to create a bond with a product was by tapping into nostalgia, a Greek word that literally means "pain from an old wound."

Draper then asks his assistant to dim the lights, adding to the drama (setting the stage). Using the very slide projector he is there to name, Draper shows a series of slides of his own family: his children playing, his pregnant wife, and a wedding photo. He speaks slowly and uses vivid language, saying, "It's not a spaceship. It's a time machine. It goes backward, forward, takes us to a place where we ache to go again. It's not called the wheel. It's a carousel; it travels like a child travels, round and round and back home again to a place where we know we are loved." Draper speaks these final words over a picture of him kissing his wife. Then a visual appears with a picture of a carousel. The lights come up, and one of Draper's fellow ad execs hurriedly leaves the meeting, about to break into tears.

Every presentation affords an opportunity to create something memorable. You are delivering a performance; rehearse several times. Be mindful of your body language, convey confidence, make eye contact. Pace yourself. Pause where necessary for dramatic effect. And always deploy some of your storytelling arsenals:

Share an anecdote, create an analogy, or get personal to provide that emotional hook. Make your audience feel something.

Engage Your Audience

A good storyteller understands that they are having a conversation with their audience. They watch for signals and listen to how the audience is reacting. Let's go back to the 2015 presidential State of the Union address to illustrate this point. President Obama was telling the story of Rebecca Erler and her family. Early in the story, the president said, "Seven years ago, Rebecca and Ben Erler were newlyweds." For some reason, someone in the chamber thought that was a notable accomplishment and applauded. That tiny little ripple of applause seemed out of place. Someone thought applauding was funny and laughed. Then another person laughed, and because President Obama was paying attention to his audience, he paused and let everyone enjoy the moment.

The laughter grew. Obama smiled and cocked his head to the side. Then everyone laughed! If you've watched a State of the Union address, you know that the vice president and the Speaker of the House sit behind the president. Joe Biden, of course, had a megawatt grin on his face as this played out. Even John Boehner, the Republican Speaker, couldn't help but grin. He tried not to smile; he didn't want to give the president the satisfaction, but he simply couldn't help it, and the corner of his lip turned up just the least little bit. This was a genuine moment where there were no Republicans and no Democrats, just a room full of people enjoying a human experience together. The only reason this scene played out is that Obama was engaged with his audience. They weren't conversing, per se, but it was a form of dialogue. And because Obama was aware of that dynamic, everyone in the room was able to enjoy a beautiful shared experience.

Color/Advance

I've written quite a bit about the science of storytelling, but it's also an art. One of the most important aspects to consider is when to double down on details and when to advance the plot of your story. By rehearsing your story and observing your test audience, you can play with this balance and see what works best. They'll help you figure out this equation simply by how they respond to the story.

Everyone knows that person who tells you *every single* detail of a story. Picture them right now. You find yourself thinking, *OK, let's move this thing along; I have to be somewhere in a couple of hours.* Then there's the person on the other end of the spectrum. They tell you what happened and that's it.

I've just described my two sisters. My younger sister never met a word she didn't like. She'll tell you about every moment in the story; then she'll introduce a sub-story, and on it goes. My older sister is the opposite. She'll tell you that she did something amazing, like overcoming a controversy in her quaint New England town after she organized a Drag Queen Story Hour at the library. But then she won't say much else. I want to know every juicy detail, and I have to drag it out of her (pun intended).

There's a wonderful improv exercise that gets at achieving this balance. It's called color/advance. In color/advance there are two individuals, a storyteller and a director. The storyteller is given a prompt: What is the craziest day you've had this year? The director's job is to say one of two words to the storyteller as they tell their story: "color" or "advance." When the director says, "Color," the storyteller must add more details to that specific moment. If they say, "Advance," the storyteller must move to the next plot point.

For example, in my older sister's case, here's how that might have gone with her Drag Queen Story Hour story. "There was lots of community excitement for the Drag Queen Story Hour. But not everyone was supportive, and when the protestors showed up to picket it, you couldn't get into the facility." "Color!" "It was a gorgeous June day, and many people held signs objecting to the event." "Advance." "I realized no one had made a safe space for our storyteller to arrive. I got a text from our storyteller, Ramona Mirage, who didn't know where to go. I made sure there was a space in our rear parking lot and arranged for Ramona to arrive at the back door away from the crowds." "Color!" You get the idea.

When crafting and practicing your stories, stay in tune with your audience, and key in on their response. Always consider this balance to keep your audience engaged.

Use Vocal Variation

"Bueller . . . Bueller . . . Bueller . . ." Ferris Bueller's economics teacher, played by Ben Stein, voiced this iconic line in the classic film *Ferris Bueller's Day Off.* Stein delivered the line in a monotone so drone-like, it's amazing that any of his students remained awake.

By comparison, Noah St. John had his audience eating out of his hand in his brilliant story "Road Trip" from NPR's acclaimed storytelling program, *Snap Judgment.* Noah won the Youth Speaks Grand Slam Championship with this story.[14]

Filmed before a live audience, Noah starts his five-minute story by saying, "When my mommas fight, they go on long car rides, and when they come back . . . the car stays still." Noah is a slight fifteen-year-old in a blue polo shirt with a mop of black hair on his head. He speaks softly, calmly, as if he's described these fights a million times before. He describes how his moms, Maria and Robin, go to separate rooms and how he listens from his room "like a radio antenna." He then starts building his story as he describes the CRV they drive. His voice grows a bit louder and gains momentum as he relays how one evening Maria asked Robin and Noah to get in the car to take a drive. Noah, convinced that this is going to be the big break-up announcement, starts to reflect on his life with his family. Anxiously, he describes the feeling of dreading the news that his parents are going to split up. You can hear the heartbreak in his voice.

Then something unexpected happens. Noah describes the turn of events, and his voice changes. There's a new energy in the timbre of his voice. He speaks a little faster, a little louder, and his voice continues to build. If you heard this story on the radio, you would

---

14   Noah St. John, "The Last Mile," NPR, Snap Judgment Performance of the Year, December 17, 2012.

be able to hear the smile in his voice. By the end, he's practically shouting as he finishes this extraordinarily well-told tale.

I'd love to tell you what makes Noah change gears, but the story is *so* good, you'll have to Google it to hear it for yourself.

Noah displays the power of vocal variety. He is the anti–Ben Stein. One of the tools that every human possesses is the ability to change the quality of their voice. Great performers are skilled at changing the character of their voice, but you don't have to be an accomplished actor, or Youth Speaks Grand Slam Champion, to be effective at it.

Think about each part of your story and make sure your voice reflects the right feeling as you develop it. If you describe a customer problem, capture the customer's frustration in your voice. Earlier, I told the story of Thibault Duchemin, the Ava app's creator, who described how his mother, father, and sister were all Deaf. He starts with a very matter-of-fact tone. But when he details their inability to follow a group conversation, you can hear the frustration in his voice: "I understand how painful it is to understand group conversations when you can't hear well. You are so focused on reading the lips in front of you when someone else starts speaking. You turn your head and miss the first words." The frustration in his voice builds: "But because you miss those words, you miss the whole conversation. Again and again and again." By sharing this story, and using his voice as an instrument, Thibault puts the audience in the customer's shoes.

Stories Work in All Cultures

I often hear from students who question whether storytelling will work in their culture. Jack Ma, Dara Khosrowshahi, and Shan-Lynn Ma are all leaders who demonstrate that storytelling is a genuinely universal experience. Jack Ma is the founder of China's Alibaba, one of the largest companies in the most populous country on the planet. Dara Khosrowshahi, an Iranian-American, runs Uber. And Shan-Lynn Ma founded one of the fastest-growing young retail companies, Zola, a bridal registry company, after she moved to the US from Australia.

During my days as a marketing executive at Yahoo! in the early 2000s, I was fortunate enough to be around some extraordinary people, and Jack Ma was one of them. Yahoo! had been one of Alibaba's biggest early investors. It was not unusual to see Ma on campus with Yahoo! cofounder Jerry Yang.

Jack is charming, humble, and persuasive. He tells a wonderful story in a *60 Minutes* interview[15] where he recalls how he was inspired to get into the internet when he visited the US as a translator in 1995. A friend in Seattle was showing him the internet, and he describes the encounter this way: "I never touched keyboard before. I never using a computer before, and I said, 'What is internet?' He said, 'Jack, just search whatever you want on the internet.' I said, 'How can I search? What does "search" mean?' He said, 'Just type.' I said, 'I don't want to type! Computer is so

---

15   Jack Ma, interviewed by Lara Logan, "Chairman Ma," *60 Minutes*, CBS, Produced by Howard Rosenburg and Julie Holstein, July 27, 2015.

expensive in China, I don't want to destroy it!' He said, 'It's not a bomb, just type.'"

Jack sits in his office in an unbuttoned sky-blue jacket with a Mandarin collar and a crisp white shirt. He's a slight man, but his eyes are so alive he appears outsized. He uses his hands to help tell the story. "So I typed the first word called 'beer.' At that time, very slow, come up American beer, Japan beer, German beer, but not Chinese beer. I was curious and type China. No China. No data. I come back to Hangzhou, one dollar in my pocket, scared, worried, and I came back and said, 'I want to do something called internet.'" He went on to build one of the world's most significant companies.

Jack grabbed his audience from his first words. "I never touched keyboard before. I never using a computer before, and I said, 'What is internet?'" Here is one of the top technology leaders on the planet, and the story starts with his fear of a keyboard. He then demonstrates many ways to tap into emotion. Jack used humor. Here's a man who created one of the ten biggest companies in the world poking fun at himself by describing his friend's reaction to his tech phobia: "It's not a bomb!" He uses a combination of pauses and animation to keep the audience hanging on his every word. He provides just enough detail to pull you into the story: "Chinese beer. No China. No data." He tells us his intent ("I want to do something called internet") and the obstacle he faces ("one dollar in my pocket").

In another famous video, he exhorts his early leadership team. In this speech, in a small, crowded room in Hangzhou, Jack creates an enemy, a classic storytelling technique. The enemy is American companies. Jack said that Americans may be good at hardware, but if his team worked hard, they could do software as well or better than the Americans. He was right.

Born in Iran, Dara Khosrowshahi fled to France with his family at the beginning of the Iranian revolution, when he was nine years old. They eventually made their way to the United States, and Dara followed his older brother to Brown University to study engineering. This proved to be a great training ground for his career as a problem-solver in business. But the most valuable course he took—that "marked me as an individual," Dara said— was European Intellectual History. "It was a tough course. Mary Gluck was a tough professor. But it really opened me up to the power of storytelling," Dara said during an interview at his alma mater in 2018. He learned how people developed philosophies, shared ideas, and changed cultures through narrative. "I've taken that into working and leadership in companies. Stories are such an incredibly powerful medium to inspire, to unite, to guide."[16]

During a different interview, Dara told a story about how he was discovered by the entertainment and internet mogul Barry Diller when he was a young analyst at the investment bank Allen and

---

16   Dara Khosrowshahi, interviewed by Brown University president, Christina Paxson, *View from the Top: Leaders in the Innovation Economy*, Brown and Beyond lecture, October 15, 2018.

Company. Diller had been working with the investment bank to launch a hostile tender offer for Paramount pictures while running QVC. "He's this *giant* Hollywood mogul." Dara raises his hands above his head as he describes the moment. "It was a dramatic offer where we'd make bids, and they'd make bids, very competitive, public battle." Dara is adding color to the background of the story so we understand how high the stakes are. "Barry would deal with an SVP, a VP, and an associate, and somehow he found out that I was running the deal model . . . and I was on the trading floor, just this nobody." Dara takes the time to introduce the setting and the characters in this story so we understand the power dynamic between the two of them.

Dara describes the encounter by "playing" Diller and himself. As he does so, he uses vocal variety to make Diller sound important and then modifies his voice to act sheepishly as he plays the younger version of himself. Diller: "You're the one who built the deal model, right?" Dara: "Yes, Mr. Diller." Diller: "I want you to explain to me *exactly* how it works." Dara: "When?" Diller: "Right now." Dara then explains what he learned from the encounter. "Barry wanted to know everything about the deal model from the person who actually built it. He really believes in going to the source. Every time you get information that's filtered, you lose fidelity in the information." In the end, Diller didn't get the deal, and Dara said his reaction was simple: "'We lost. They won. Next.' I wanted to be part of next."[17] Diller hired Dara, and

---

17   Dara Khosrowshahi, interviewed by Lepi Jha Fishman, *View from the Top*, Stanford University Graduate School of Business, December 3, 2018.

he ultimately ran Expedia, one of Diller's companies. Dara shared something he learned from the experience: Get information from the source and keep moving forward. This simple, well-chosen anecdote taught us a lot about Dara and what he values. When he took over the leadership of Uber in 2017, Dara used those storytelling skills to galvanize his organization and shepherd a much-needed change in culture for the company.

I recruited Shan-Lyn Ma out of Stanford Business School to work on my marketing team at Yahoo! in 2006. She was extremely sharp, motivated, and charming. Years later, Shan-Lyn went on to create the bridal registry powerhouse Zola.

"When I was growing up, I was not like other little girls,"[18] Shan-Lyn explained at an industry event in 2017. "Many of my friends wanted to be pilots or astronauts, or fire-fighters or teachers." She continues, "I wanted to be Jerry Yang, the cofounder of Yahoo!." Shan-Lyn commands the dais at an industry event where she is promoting Zola. "He set the stage for Google and Facebook, and I idolized Jerry and wanted to be like Jerry. Looking at him, I saw another immigrant who started with very little but worked very hard and now has a lasting impact on the world." Shan-Lyn is weaving a tale that describes the arc of her origin story, from her beginnings as a Chinese Australian girl to one of the leading

---

18   Shan-Lyn Ma, *The Hustle*, Hustle-Con 2017, July 26, 2017.

women tech founders in America. She's also subtly using the technique of sharing an analog. She was effectively saying, *Here's this immigrant (Jerry) who came to America to create an amazing innovation, and now you're hearing from another immigrant (me) who's come to America to do the same.*

"I saw that Jerry and other Silicon Valley founders had gone to Stanford, so I went to Stanford for my MBA, and of course I went [on] to Yahoo!. My best day was when I passed Jerry Yang in the corridor. He didn't see me, but I saw him, and I silently freaked out." Anyone who has ever seen their idol in person can relate to this story. Shan-Lyn is sharing a moment, which helps her audience understand her aspiration to follow in his substantial footsteps. As of 2017, Shan-Lyn had never properly met Jerry or spoken to him. But that would soon change. Not only did he meet and talk with Shan-Lynn, Jerry also became an investor in the bridal registry company that she founded. His investment was part of the $100M she raised to grow her extraordinary company.

Everyone Wants to Tell a Great Story

You've learned that your objective as a storyteller is to persuade your audience. If you're memorable, compelling, and clear, there's a high chance the listener will become intrigued by your innovation and tell someone about it. That's your ultimate goal. If you're meeting with an investor, you'll want them to tell their partners so they'll invest. If you're speaking with a prospective employee, you'll want her to share the story with her partner, family, or friends and decide to work for you. If you're speaking with a customer, you want him to pass this great idea on to other potential customers.

To show the power of a good story, I'm going to share a story with you that I heard from Alex, who heard it from Chris after he met with Kevin.[19] The best stories are easy to pass along.

Alex Blumberg, a producer for NPR who covers business stories, recently became an entrepreneur himself by developing a podcast platform. Along the way, Alex sought the advice of Chris Sacca, a billionaire venture capitalist whose homerun early-stage investments include Twitter, Uber, and Instagram. Chris is a smart guy and a great judge of entrepreneurial talent.

Chris told Alex the following story, which I heard on NPR. One day, Chris received a call from a colleague asking him to meet with Kevin Systrom, the founder of a startup called Instagram. Chris wasn't really interested. He had already made some money from an investment in another photo-sharing company, and Chris thought the photo-sharing space was saturated. But he met with Kevin as a favor to the colleague.

In the meeting, Chris was blown away by Kevin's vision. It was 2010, and Kevin described how everyone has this new thing in their pocket that doubles as a camera. Remember, it was still the early days of the smartphone. At that point, most photo-sharing happened on a desktop computer. Systrom said the process needed to be optimized on the move, on your phone. His new creation, Instagram, made that possible.

---

19 Alex Blumberg, "How Not to Pitch a Billionaire," *StartUp Podcast*, Gimlet Media, Episode 1, September 5, 2014.

Chris said, "As you listen to him, you get the perception that he's actually looking *through* you to some spot behind you five years into the future. He *knows* the inevitability of the success of his platform. At the end of the conversation, you're like, please take my money!" Chris made it clear that Kevin showed a quality that investors always look for in great entrepreneurs: conviction. *Extreme* conviction. Despite his doubts going in, Chris invested in Instagram, and Instagram later sold to Facebook for $1B.

A great story is one that everyone can retell, that they *want* to retell. It should be simple, clear, and compelling. After all, if you want your audience to embrace your new idea, they must first remember, understand, and be motivated by your story. And yes, conviction goes a long way toward making that happen. If you tell a good story well, your audience will probably pass the story on. That's when you win!

>>>→

Act 3

How to Level-Up Your Story

8

Story Archetypes

We've covered the basics of building and telling a compelling story. Now let's level up and explore different story archetypes. Some writers believe there are only a small number of stories in the world, and every story is some version of these story archetypes. In his seminal book, *The Seven Basic Plots: Why We Tell Stories*, the controversial author and journalist Christopher Booker writes that every story follows one of seven patterns:

- Overcoming the monster

- Rags to riches

- The quest

- Voyage and return

- Rebirth

- Comedy

- Tragedy

Whether you agree with Booker's analysis or not, it does reveal a certain truth about stories. Most stories are familiar because they draw on a structure and tropes that we can easily identify.

Similarly, a number of themes present themselves repeatedly in innovation narratives, and I share seven of these story archetypes here.

1. The Inevitable, Meaningful Change

The last story I told at the end of Act 2 was about the power of Kevin Systrom's conviction in pitching Instagram to future investor Chris Sacca. It was about the viral nature of stories. The best ones get passed along. But it was *also* about another powerful idea for the storyteller: the inevitable, meaningful change. If a trend is so powerful that its inevitability is a given, the storyteller has discovered a little gold mine. The change that Kevin talked about with Chris was how people took and manipulated photographs.

In 2010, the smartphone was just a few years old, and though people were beginning to use it as a camera, it had not yet evolved into the primary camera for most people. As a result, most photo-sharing applications were web-based, because you took photos with a camera and transferred them to your computer. Chris, the Instagram investor who told the story about Kevin's pitch, initially passed on the meeting altogether. He'd already made some money on Photobucket, another photo-sharing service, and he was ready to move on to other categories. In his mind, the photo-sharing category was crowded, and there wasn't any fertile ground left to cultivate.

But Kevin impressed Chris with the inevitable, meaningful change that would take place in terms of how people took photos. Kevin showed Chris his smartphone and effectively said, "Look, *this* is what people will use to take photos in the future . . . and *this* is what people are going to want to use to optimize and share them."

If you bought that version of the future—if you believed that such an inevitable, meaningful change was about to take place— you were well on your way to understanding that Instagram would be a hit. Chris did. And it was.

One powerful storytelling strategy, then, is to lead with the inevitable, meaningful change. Describe where the world is going, emphasize the certainty about this trend, and then place your product or service right in the middle of that new world.

Coreshell Technologies used this strategy in a recent SkyDeck Accelerator demo-day presentation. Coreshell founder, Jonathan Tan, began by describing the global demand for long-lasting batteries as we move to more sustainable energy sources like electric cars. It was a compelling case about the future of mobility. Jonathan then described how his team created a technology to enable battery makers to make longer-lasting batteries. They've devised a coating that can increase battery capacity and lifetime by 50 percent and is 25 percent cheaper to produce. If you are convinced that batteries will increasingly power the world and that Coreshell's technology does what Jonathan says it can, then you're convinced that you have to learn more about Coreshell. Jonathan has done his job as a storyteller by compelling you to gain a deeper understanding of his company. His presentation was effective, as it led to the raise of a $4M seed round.

2. The Shared-Purpose Narrative

From Fighting Crimes to Changing Communities

Ralph Clark had a deep sense of purpose when he joined ShotSpotter, a gunshot-detection solution company, in 2010. As a Black man who grew up in East Oakland, California, he understood the impact his company could have on communities like the one where he grew up. But he knew that his purpose had to be shared by his employees if the company was to take off. ShotSpotter had been around for years and enjoyed slow and steady growth. Ralph set out to accelerate ShotSpotter's trajectory with the ultimate goal of taking the company public.

On its surface, ShotSpotter helps local law enforcement detect, identify, and follow up on gunshots in their communities. For some time, police departments considered ShotSpotter a useful tool primarily if it could help them solve more crimes. Police chiefs chose to evaluate its effectiveness solely through that lens. But by early 2017, it was clear that ShotSpotter had an even more meaningful role to play in American cities.

The Black Lives Matter movement had hit its stride after the riots in Ferguson, Missouri, just two and a half years prior. The relationship between marginalized urban communities (especially Black and Brown) and local police forces had deteriorated to one of the lowest points since the civil rights protests of the 1960s. Communities were justifiably upset, and police chiefs struggled to reestablish relationships with the communities they were supposed to protect and serve.

Ralph knew that ShotSpotter could play a role in helping to bridge the divide. He made it a priority to better articulate this shared-purpose story to motivate his team and engage new customers.

One of the worst things that can happen in any neighborhood is the outbreak of gun violence. If someone fired a gun in front of my home, I'm confident the police would respond in minutes. But in the most marginalized communities in America like East Oakland (which is only fifteen miles away from my home), only 20 percent of gunshots are reported. Imagine living in a community where 80 percent of the time that a gun is fired, the police don't show up. Would you feel as if you mattered to the police? There are many reasons why no one reports gunshots (e.g., fear of retribution), but the bottom line is that the police force is unable to respond if they don't know the shots were fired in the first place. This promotes further distrust in the community. The frustration and anger raised by the Black Lives Matter movement only exacerbated this divide.

But Ralph believed that ShotSpotter could change the narrative. If the police can respond to *every* gunshot, then members of the community will feel more respected. In progressive police circles, this is called procedural justice. It opens up lines of communication with the neighborhood and helps the police identify the handful of people behind the vast majority of the shootings. The police, in turn, engage in strategies of focused deterrence with these individuals to get guns out of their hands. These strategies can dramatically reduce gun violence and improve the confidence the community has in the police. This is a powerful shared-purpose narrative.

ShotSpotter was recently featured in a customer testimonial video from a company called TriNet, which ShotSpotter uses to support several HR functions. As part of their "People Matter" campaign, TriNet asked ShotSpotter employees to write Ralph a letter that conveyed this purpose:

> Gun violence has become a daily occurrence in our nation. And it can feel like we've become numb to its existence. Every time a gunshot goes unreported and unaddressed, community members are left to think that their lives aren't valued. We are changing this perception of law enforcement to serve more equitably. By combining the power of acoustic sensors with machine learning,

we can detect and report gunfire with unparalleled speed and precision. We never lose sight of our goal—to help provide equal protection for all. We are a diverse team who are passionate about our mission, to proactively engage police, community members, and city leaders in reducing gun violence. And we are honored to make such a life-changing difference for so many people simply by doing our jobs.[20]

The lesson in this purpose narrative is that Ralph didn't stop with his discovery about why he went to work every day. He took the time to think about it, developed the narrative, and then made sure his team understood and embraced it. Obviously, this same narrative has resonated with customers and investors alike. ShotSpotter continues to thrive as a company and build value. As of this writing, the stock has more than tripled since its IPO three years ago, and the company continues to make a difference in local communities throughout the US and cities around the world.

Lime Sustains its Mission-Driven Narrative

Brad Bao, the cofounder and chairman of the micro-mobility company Lime, told me that maintaining a shared mission and purpose for his fast-growing global company was his biggest challenge.

---

20 TriNet, "People Matter" customer testimonial campaign featuring ShotSpotter, *People Who Champion a Mission Matter.*

"How do we maintain an inclusive culture when we're expanding rapidly across different geographies and cultures?" Brad's network of lime-colored shared electric bikes and scooters have become ubiquitous in cities around the world, leading to explosive growth for the company and changing the way people travel. "I used to interview every candidate and attend all new employee orientations. That's harder to do now with hundreds of team members all over the world." Brad had always envisioned a company that helped to make cities more livable, is a great place to work, and fosters the right values. And more importantly. he needed to find a way for his employees to internalize this as well.

I hired Brad as an intern at Yahoo! when he was in business school. Sixteen years later, he's the co-founder and chairman of a $2.4 billion company. Over Korean food at Lime's San Francisco headquarters recently, Brad told me that a piece of advice I gave him early in his career had stayed with him. He was a recent immigrant from China and knew little of American business culture back then. I suggested he follow a simple rule: "Be authentic. Be true to what you believe in. And tell everyone about it." Brad said my advice has been his North Star ever since.

Brad and his cofounder, Toby Sun, started Lime in 2017, and they've stayed true to their ideals, even when decisions flew in the face of conventional startup wisdom. For example, it was customary for many startups to helicopter into new cities without engaging the local authorities. However, Brad felt that the only way to stay true to the mission and achieve his vision was to collaborate with municipalities and local communities. Lime patiently worked with cities to establish regulations and obtained permits before any launch. They also engaged local communities as they crafted safety education campaigns. Moreover, he committed Lime to provide bikes and scooters to residents who did not have smartphones or credit cards; other mobility companies wouldn't waste their time with that. Furthermore, he opened markets in Europe before fully establishing Lime in the US.

Many were skeptical, but Brad stuck to his guns because he had a sense of purpose to build a thriving, long-term company that mitigates traffic and pollution and makes city-living more fun.

Now, one of Brad's top priorities is ensuring his employees share those values. To bring this vision to life for customers and employees alike, Lime created a communications campaign featuring community members (not actors) of diverse backgrounds and abilities. The campaign conveyed this purpose narrative about improving city life. One video features Carlos, the son of Salvadorans, now living on the south side of LA. In it, Carlos says that it used to take forever to get anywhere in the city using buses and trains, so he tended to stay in his neighborhood. "You're stuck in a box, you know. There's no connection to the outside." But when Lime came to his neighborhood, all of that changed. "When I get in a Scooter, the whole world opens up . . . sometimes I ride all the way to the beach." He now sees parts of LA he'd never seen before and feels less like an outsider and more a part of his city.

Brad takes pride in the fact that Lime's values have taken root. He points out that even Lime alums who have gone on to build companies of their own are creating mission-driven cultures rooted in shared values. They have learned that a strong purpose narrative enables a company to have everyone rowing—or in this case, riding—in the same direction.

The Mighty Mission

Throughout the book, I've shared stories of innovators with a profound purpose. Surbhi Sarna committed to making strides in early ovarian cancer detection. Michelle Crosby wanted to make the process of divorce a little less painful for couples and their children. Thibault Duchemin wanted to make it easier for those who cannot hear to follow a group conversation. A strong purpose can inspire employees, investors, and partners. By sharing your mission through a compelling story, you can galvanize the community of supporters you'll need to make it happen.

3. The Crisis Story

The Day the Novel Coronavirus Got Our Attention

On Wednesday, March 11, 2020, my day started with an ordinary conference call. I spoke with the leaders of the American Conservatory Theater in San Francisco, where I serve as board chair. We were concerned about the impact of COVID-19 on our community but hadn't yet made specific plans to close our theaters. By the end of the day, that all changed. The *world* changed.

To put this moment in context, the Golden State Warriors held a basketball game the night before in San Francisco with over fifteen thousand people in attendance. I was there. Think about that. By March 11, there were already 118,000 documented cases globally and 4,296 deaths from the virus. Vast regions of China had been shuttered for a couple of months. There was concern in the United States, but we hadn't dramatically changed our behaviors yet.

But the next evening, while I was at the theater surrounded by hundreds of people, our news feeds started to buzz. "Tom Hanks and his wife, Rita Wilson, have tested positive for the coronavirus." And a bit later, "Rudi Gobert of the Utah Jazz has also tested positive. The NBA is suspending the season."

In a moment, this faceless threat had a face. It had a few faces. We now *knew* the characters in the story. In fact, the leading character, Hanks, was one of the most beloved personalities in the country. Until that point, we just had data and logic, but we didn't have an emotional narrative. With the narrative taking hold, however, a series of dominos began to fall.

By the end of the evening, this story had changed our world and just about everyone else's too. The governor of California announced a limit on gatherings of more than 250 people. We shut down our shows at the theater.

The next day, the American president started to take the threat more seriously. Within a couple of days, schools began sending students home for online classes. A couple of days after that, the entire Bay Area found itself under a shelter-in-place order. One week after allowing fifteen thousand people to attend a basketball game, San

Francisco told its residents they had to stay home unless they absolutely had to go out. It was the first place in America to do so.

"I think data is far more powerful than emotion for a lot of people," one of my students said recently. Data *is* powerful. The data Americans had on March 11 *was* powerful. We knew that over one hundred thousand people globally had contracted a potentially fatal illness and that over four thousand souls lost their lives. But without a story—without a face—that data did not resonate with the vast majority of Americans. We now know plenty of smart people advised American leaders to take more severe action much earlier, but it didn't happen. Once there was a story, that powerful data took on more meaning.

This is a crisis story. Many innovations emerged from this moment, including new methods for making emergency equipment such as masks and ventilators; new protocols for everyday activities such as grocery shopping; and new ways of holding meetings and teaching classes.

There are two points to take away from this example: (1) Great innovations often emerge from a crisis, and that narrative can be powerful, and (2) unless you tell a good story, sometimes even a crisis won't be enough to launch your new idea. The impact of our COVID-19 experience illustrates the power of a relatable story to break through the noise of our busy lives—to grab us and get us to pay attention.

Winston Churchill famously said, "Never waste a good crisis." President Obama was adhering to that notion when he tried to help Americans retool after the 2008 financial crisis. The story he told about Rebekah and Ben Erler at the 2015 State of the Union address was a crisis story. He shared how they navigated the Great Recession through the help of government-funded initiatives.

This book has been all about innovation, where the focus is a product, service, or program. But sometimes you face a personal crisis and find that *you* are the focus of the innovation. You need to reinvent yourself. You also might find a moment when you have to inspire your team to change. By showing vulnerability, a leader can inspire others to follow them on a difficult path. The following is a story that grew out of a personal crisis and finally led its protagonist to an unexpected moment of vulnerability.

Lance Armstrong Understands

Lance Armstrong is one of the most polarizing sports figures of his generation. He won seven Tour de France titles between 1998 and 2005 after recovering from testicular cancer earlier in the '90s. He was idolized by cycling fans and adored by most Americans for dominating a predominantly European sport. But at the end of his cycling career, the authorities stripped him of every title, and his reputation was destroyed by his drug use. Armstrong doped, he said, because all the elite cycling athletes of his era did, but that didn't matter to most observers. Armstrong had cheated, and people were horrified by his many years of denying it as well as his verbal attacks on people who suggested otherwise.

Lance finally admitted his use of performance-enhancing substances in an interview with Oprah Winfrey in 2013. And it wasn't until several years after that when he properly owned what he'd done and expressed true contrition for doing so.

Recently, Armstrong did something uncharacteristic. He showed real vulnerability. During the radio program *Freakonomics* on NPR in 2018, Armstrong told the following story.[21] He had been staying at an Airbnb in Denver, Colorado, to attend the Colorado Classic bike race. His Airbnb was across from some brewpubs, and he had called an Uber to pick him up to take him to the race. The Uber driver parked directly in front of a patio of partiers. As he's walking across the street to his car, Lance sees that he's been noticed by someone in the crowd. If you're Lance Armstrong, you're quite used to this. Lance recalls the moment this way:

"This one guy goes, 'Hey, Lance!' And I fully expected him to say, 'What's up, dude? Right on. Love ya!' And I go, 'Hey, what's up?' And he says, 'Fuck you! Fuck you! Fuck you!' And he wouldn't stop. And the next thing you know, the *entire* patio is screaming, 'Fuck you! Fuck you! Fuck you!'"

Armstrong pauses and says to the interviewer, "Steve, I never had that happen. I was *shaking*." He pauses to collect himself. "So, I got in the car . . . and I'm saying to myself, 'You're Lance Armstrong. You have to *do* something.' So, I called the bar. I said, 'Put the manager on the phone.' I explain everything that happened. He says, 'Oh man, I'm so sorry, dude.' I said, 'OK, I need you to do me a favor. Here's my credit card number. I want you

---

21   Lance Armstrong, interview by Steven Dubner, "Has Lance Armstrong Finally Come Clean?" *Freakonomics*, episode 342, Produced by Derek John, July 25, 2018.

to walk out there and buy everything they're eating and drinking. And tell them . . . tell them . . . that I understand.'"

Armstrong's default mode is extreme cockiness; he's fiercely competitive and a bully. It was only after years of listening to his followers that he started to change. He discovered that his supporters felt duped by what they saw as a false narrative. Those who worked with him on his Livestrong cancer foundation even told him they felt somehow complicit in the deception. Armstrong faced a personal crisis, and it was only through years of self-discovery that he was able to show remorse and genuine contrition. By sharing this story, Armstrong made himself vulnerable and garnered respect from some of the doubters who thought he would never learn from his mistakes. If you're trying to get others on your team to learn from their mistakes, demonstrate some vulnerability of your own.

4. The Promised Land Story

A fellow business storyteller, Andy Raskin, touts a useful tool for storytelling called the Promised Land strategy. Innovators paint a picture of two worlds: the one we're in and the one we *could* be in. The one we could be in is better and brighter than the one in which we're currently living. The innovator's product or service then becomes the catalyst to create the future world.

Chipotle restaurants created *The Scarecrow* to tell a powerful Promised Land story. *The Scarecrow*, an animated short video from Chipotle, features a scarecrow who works as a handyman in the

Crow Foods Incorporated factory. The dark, depressing place uses inhumane methods to raise and process beef, pork, and poultry. The scarecrow is horrified by the way they treat cows, pigs, and chicken. The animation is filmed with a sepia-toned wash to convey a post-apocalyptic world, with Fiona Apple singing an anguished cover of "Pure Imagination" from *Willy Wonka and the Chocolate Factory*. Effectively, Chipotle said, "This is how food is made in our current world, and it's not pretty." After watching the video, you long for something better.

We find the Promised Land in the second half of the video when the scarecrow returns home after work. He discovers a brilliant red pepper on a plant in his garden and picks it. He then harvests corn and other fresh ingredients. The music brightens; the sky turns from yellow to blue. The scarecrow drives his truck back into town, and in the shadow of the Crow Foods factory, he starts to prepare fresh food in a small stall. The music swells, and Fiona Apple sings, "You want to change the world . . . there's nothing to it." A nearby customer peers over at the scarecrow's stand, and a small smile curls up on his face as he approaches. Chipotle has created its Promised Land. Chipotle is now saying that "fast-food can actually be created from fresh and sustainably sourced ingredients." A banner drops down above the scarecrow's shop that reads, "Cultivate a better world."

Chipotle told a Promised Land story. It shared a world that's ugly and replaced it with the kind of world you'd want to live in. Their product is the bridge that takes you there.

The company Databricks emerged from an open-source data platform called Apache Spark, which Matei Zaharia created while working on his PhD. In 2014, Matei partnered with his professor, Ion Stoica, and fellow grad student Ali Ghodsi to found Databricks to build products and services on top of Apache Spark. Ghodsi is CEO of the company today.

I worked with the three of them when they started out in a tiny office in downtown Berkeley. They were developing a story for the company, and we created a Promised Land narrative.

The protagonist was a data scientist working in a growing tech company. Executives in the company had been making considerable investments in big data under the premise that they could extract valuable insights from all the data they collected. In this Promised Land view, the company would enjoy huge advantages if they could understand their customers and what makes them tick better than their competitors could. Executives would take these insights, apply them to their products, and win big in the marketplace. All the company had to do was hire talented data scientists and let them do their magic to unearth the insights. In this version of the world, the data scientist could be the company's superhero.

That's the Promised Land view. It turns out, however, that the reality looks nothing like that. The real story is that the data scientist effectively operates while wearing shackles. Building and running experiments is a nightmare because of the complexity of these big data systems and the dearth of decent tools.

The current view of the world looks nothing like the Promised Land view. Our job as storytellers was to tell how Databricks could turn that data scientist into the company superhero by giving him the tools to deliver that Promised Land. I'll describe precisely how they did so later in the book.

The exciting news is that Databricks is delivering on this Promised Land story. In six years, Databricks grew from three guys in a tiny office to a 1,400-person company currently valued at $38B. They grew at this remarkable pace because they created a true Promised Land for data scientists everywhere.

I've shared other Promised Land stories in this book. Blackberry painted the picture of a fantastical Promised Land where executives could read and write emails regardless of where they were. Jennifer Hyman and Jennifer Fleiss pictured a Promised Land where a special-occasion designer dress was never out of reach for a working woman. And the folks at Huggies created a Promised Land where parents of toddlers who were still potty training would never be embarrassed for their children or themselves again. If you can imagine that future, and get people excited about the vision, it can take you a long way in building the followers you'll need to get there.

5. The Two-Sided Market (a Love Story!)

Two-sided markets create a unique storytelling challenge. Here, the innovator connects two parties, each of whom needs something that the other provides. Think Airbnb: where travelers look for a cool place to stay and homeowners or renters try to make a few extra bucks from unused rooms. Komal Ahmad's Copia connects hungry Americans with institutions that would otherwise throw out their excess food. Party A needs party B. To get what they want they must come together in some way. It's a love story.

The film *Crazy Rich Asians* is a classic love story. Nick Young and Rachel Chu could not be any more different. Although they are both college professors at NYU, Nick comes from one of the richest families in Singapore, and Rachel is the daughter of an immigrant single mother living in Queens, New York. When over dinner Rachel tells the family of her Singaporean friend Peik Lin that her boyfriend's name is Nick Young, they spit the food back onto their plates. Rachel asks if they know who Nick is. Peik Lin's father exclaims, "Who doesn't know who they are? They're just the biggest developers in Singapore, Malaysia, Thailand, Brunei, . . . New Mexico."

Throughout the movie, the chemistry between these two beautiful people is palpable, but the difference in their status threatens to rip their relationship apart. In a powerful scene, Nick's mother, Eleanor, confronts Rachel about Rachel's own mother's past, which Eleanor discovered by hiring a private detective. Rachel glares at Eleanor and says, "I don't want any part of your family," before storming off.

This beautiful relationship looks as if it could never last.

But thanks to her cleverness and brilliant mind, Rachel eventually wins over Nick's family. The journey is particularly satisfying for the audience because we get to know Nick and Rachel both so well. As viewers of this relationship odyssey, we are desperate to find out how this unlikely match will work.

Any innovation that brings together two sides of a market is a little like *Crazy Rich Asians*. It's a love story. To fully grasp the power of the idea, the innovator must convey who the two sets of customers are, what they both want, and how the new service is going to somehow find a way to put them together.

Uber is a classic example. When we think of the Uber customer, we typically think of passengers who wish they had a better way to get around town. There are a million things they hate about taxis. They hate waiting around for a cab, wondering if it's going to come, dreading that they might get a dirty cab or a lousy driver, and not knowing if they'll have enough cash to cover the fare.

This was a huge set of problems to solve, and Travis Kalanick and Garrett Camp, Uber's cofounders, knew they needed another group of people to fix it. They needed people who found the emerging gig economy appealing. People who had some free time and hoped to find a convenient way to make some money. These people also had an asset—their car—that was underutilized. The founders asked, What if we could put this unlikely set of people together to find a solution? It was a true love story that resulted in Uber.

Verto Education is a brand-new two-sided market story. Verto brings together graduating high school seniors looking to take some time off with universities interested in better managing their enrollment. To create this business, Verto Ed had to build a compelling narrative for *both* parties.

A Gap Year That Works for Everybody

Verto's founder and CEO, Mitch Gordon, had already founded one company, GoOverseas.com, in the travel/education category. This experience led to an interesting discovery. Mitch realized that eighteen-year-olds who enjoyed international travel during a gap year had some frustrations with the process. They loved the experience and felt they needed the time to mature before college, but they disliked the additional cost and time commitment of that extra year. They wished there was a way to do an international gap year, be assured that they would get into a competitive college, and still finish school in the original four years.

Meanwhile, Mitch also realized that higher education was struggling. Competition for top students was accelerating, and coding boot camps and online courses were offering more affordable options. The cost of a degree was skyrocketing, and many families pondered whether college was still worth the price. In addition, most universities could not replace the students that dropped out after freshman year. The national average for freshman retention in higher ed is 75 percent. This means they need to replace one-quarter of the student body the next year with transfer students. Only the most elite schools have an easy time filling up a sophomore class with transfers. Universities wished they had a ready-made cohort of smart, well-adjusted students to slot into their sophomore class every year.

If this sounds like a love story in the making, you've been paying attention! Verto Education created a marketplace to put these two sets of customers together. They built a program that allows students to simultaneously apply for an international gap year program *and* entrance to a leading university. Once accepted, the student enjoys an international experience and receives a full year of credit from the university that accepted them. When they complete their gap year of international travel, they have only three years of proper university left to go!

6. The Pivot Story

Sometimes a story takes an unexpected turn. If it's an improvement, you need to embrace it! The first innovation narrative you create is only a hypothesis until you test it with your customer, the protagonist in your story. If your story resonates, great! But if you need to tweak it or make a significant pivot because you discover a better narrative, then do it. Just revise your storyboard; you should be happy to do so before you sink too much time and money into the lesser idea. Your innovation narrative now becomes a strategic tool. The story pivot itself can also be useful in sharing your story. You talk about where you started and how a customer discovery led you to where you ended up.

Anything but Craigslist

Entrepreneurs Ben Hamlin and Maya Tobias happily rewrote their story. If you speak to anyone who runs a small business with part-time employees, they'll probably tell you that the least favorite part of their job is hiring them. Ben and Maya heard that over and over again as they talked to prospective customers about their startup idea, Localwise.

Ben and Maya, friends from Berkeley-Haas business school,

grew up in families that ran small businesses. Because small companies are always looking for professional services (bookkeepers, designers, etc.), they saw a need for a Yelp-like service just for businesses. They started building a product called Localwise and went out to talk to business owners about it. They were testing the hypothesis for their new idea by vetting their innovation narrative.

But while speaking with these small businesses and trying to understand their biggest pain points, they kept hearing, "We *hate* Craigslist as a local hiring solution." They felt the quality of applicants was spotty and the experience clunky. Through these conversations, Ben and Maya discovered a *greater* problem to solve, and they completely changed their narrative. Localwise matches local businesses and part-time employees, most of which are students. They simply found people needed a job-matching service more, which changed the narrative, and they ran with that new story. Today Localwise continues to grow, with over sixty thousand local employers offering jobs on its site operating in cities across America.

Story pivots are extremely common in the innovation world. It's more likely than not that you'll make a significant shift in your story, as long as you're spending time with your prospective customers. By listening to your customers, you are gaining a deeper connection with the protagonist in your story. That richer understanding informs everything else in the story, including the innovation itself. And by *telling* the story of your discovery and pivot, you're sharing how well you understand your customer.

The B2C to B2B Pivot Story

Another common story pivot is the shift from a business-to-consumer (B2C) model to a business-to-business (B2B) model or vice versa. One example, Rize, initially made a consumer financial app before pivoting to create apps for banks.

Dash Robotics also changed course. A product development studio, Dash creates robotics products primarily for the toy industry. When I met founders Nick Kohut, Andrew Gillies, and Paul Birkmeyer, they were building a great narrative. A team of mechanical engineers, they set out to create a cool new toy robot that children could assemble themselves. As we talked about their developing story, we focused on the child-parent relationship. Kids want to have fun, while their parents want them to play outside away from screens and learn something. The original Dash robot, which they later called the Kamigami robot, was a robotic toy bug that kids could build, program, and operate with a mobile device. Dash had a strong narrative, early funders, and the beginning of a business.

Over time, however, the Dash team learned that penetrating the toy business was a long, hard slog, with lengthy lead times to prepare for the holiday season. They gained traction, but along the way, they realized they were more interested in making great robots than building a consumer business. So, they pivoted.

Dash realized that there was another customer narrative they could attack. It turns out that toy companies are great at building a consumer business, but not so skilled at building robots. They had tremendous properties, such as Trolls, Hot Wheels, and

Jurassic Park, but they needed help creating dynamic new toys for these franchises. Dash shifted their focus to include this new protagonist (the toy companies), figured out where the companies needed help, and decided to become a development studio. They changed from a B2C story to a B2B story. They've since created toys for Mattel, Hasbro, and WowWee, among others. In telling this story, the innovator shares their knowledge of the end user (their new customer's customer) and what's important to them. By describing your pivot, you're revealing the discovery of the customer need.

7. The "You Changed My Life" Story

Mr. K99397

"My name is Jason Spyres. It's nice to be able to use that name, because for many years, the only name that mattered in my life was Mr. K99397. That was my prison number."

Jason is a white man with a shock of brown hair and piercing eyes. He looks considerably older than most college students, but he's sitting in an empty classroom, looking into a camera, and telling a remarkable story. His intention is simply to share his experience and thank the organization that matters to him. But he's actually telling a "you changed my life" story. When you, as the innovator, already have customers using your product, you just might discover a treasure like this. A story that says everything anyone needs to hear about your product.

Jason continues: "Unfortunately, at a young age, I made a stupid decision to sell cannabis, and I ended up in prison. I was never really good at school. . . . I was smart, but I couldn't focus . . . not to make excuses . . . but my parents had drug addictions, I didn't have the best guidance . . . but I own up to my own choices." He pauses and reflects. Jason then describes how his fortunes slowly started to turn. His mother and father addressed their addictions and turned to helping their son. He decided to improve his education, and his mother sent him Khan Academy transcripts to get him started.

Khan founder Sal Khan was speaking on a college campus when he met Jason. Sal heard Jason's story and asked him to share it with him on camera. It was the perfect story to convey the narrative of Khan Academy. From his work with the transcripts of Khan classes, Jason discovered that he understood how fractions worked, was good with numbers, and ultimately could test well. He learned complex math equations that improved his SAT performance. Jason took a work-release program that enabled him to go to community college, take the standardized tests, and apply to transfer to a university.

Thanks to the Khan videos and his hard work, Jason was accepted to Stanford. Just a year later, Jason found himself in a classroom with Sal Khan as the guest speaker. "I got to tell him—" Jason tears up a bit. "Thank you. Thank you for playing a role in me now being a Stanford University student studying computer science after being locked up for fifteen years without access to technology."[22]

---

22 Jason Spyres testimonial, Khan Academy customer, featured in an email from Khan founder Sal Khan, "I'm not crying, you're crying," accessible on emailtuna. com/khanacademy.org.

Now we know where this extraordinary story is going, but we don't yet have the full arc of the story. Exactly how did Khan Academy give Jason what he needed? Again, if we keep listening, we'll get that part of the story too.

The Khan Academy videos were easy to understand, and Jason was able to study "without having to admit 'I'm stupid' if I didn't already know it; it took away the embarrassment factor of having to ask someone else."

He closes with a statement that *is* the value proposition for Khan Academy. You literally could not have scripted Jason's heartfelt comment any better: "There's so many other people that have the potential to make my story nothing if they can just get their *hands on the ability to learn.*"

Innovators find that the need to tell their story never really goes away—even after they raise the early money and launch the product. When your product is a bit more established, you will have customers. Listen to them, and they may just share the perfect story of their experience to enable you to tell yours.

Where to Take the Story from Here

When is your story finished? How can you be confident that your story will resonate with your audience? The truth is that a story is never truly finished. It's a living, breathing entity that you should continue refining. Every time you tell your story, there's a chance to make it a little better.

I've written quite a bit about Pixar's process because story-making *is* their business. They dedicate years to building the story before their final push into production, which typically takes about a year. At that point, they enlist a multitude of artists to fully realize the film. But even in those last moments of creation, the final touches can make all the difference in the world.

Take *Toy Story 4*. You can argue that the movie should never have been made. In fact, many people, including certain people at

Pixar, felt that way. The trilogy that ended with the phenomenal *Toy Story 3* seemed just about perfect. Andy, the boy who plays with Woody and Buzz all his life, grows up during the first two films and heads off to college in the third. In *Toy Story 3*, the toys must find a new child, Bonnie, which provides the perfect narrative arc to the trilogy. But *Toy Story* is such a massive franchise for Pixar's parent company, Disney, that there was too much pressure to do another one.

Fast-forward to the development of *Toy Story 4*. Insiders worried that they couldn't pull it off. Several Pixar artists feared that the story wasn't strong enough to carry the movie. *Toy Story 4*'s plot centers on a new character, Forky. Woody's new owner, Bonnie, created Forky in kindergarten out of a spork. Poor Forky thinks he's garbage and tries to throw himself away. Woody sets out to save him, and they're off on an adventure. But the movie is really about Woody, no longer the most important toy in Bonnie's life. How will Woody come to terms with that?

Despite improvements during the story-building process, several insiders thought the film would never be great. But once Pixar's brilliant animators and set designers created their final magic, attitudes started changing. The animators and visual designers conveyed the toys' emotions in such an extraordinary way that the story clicked into place. This was especially true in the climactic scenes when Woody is debating whether he should stay with his lifelong toy buddies or set off on a new adventure of his own.

In one memorable scene, Woody says goodbye to his old friend Bo Peep, with whom he briefly reunites during the film. It is as poignant as any great scene featuring two live actors. Standing atop a merry-go-round at a town fair, both characters shift their eyes to the ground, then look up at each other as Bo says, "I'm glad I got to see you again." She moves in for a warm embrace, and Woody shuts his eyes. As Woody turns to leave, Bo steps forward, and with a beautiful sadness on her face, she straightens Woody's cowboy hat and touches his cheek before he whispers, "Goodbye, Bo," and sets off. It's an extraordinary moment and delivers all the emotional punch the story needs. Through constant refinement and attention to detail, the Pixar gang pulled it off. *Toy Story 4* became a huge hit and won the Academy Award for best animated feature in 2020.

OK, you're not making a movie, but you, too, can continue polishing your story. Nuance matters. You might discover a turn of phrase, a better visual of the problem, or a way to convey the product demo that brings everything together.

Steve Derico is the founder of Dottie, a startup that is making it easier for cancer patients and their families to manage their care. In discussing the Dottie story with Steve over Zoom during the pandemic, we stumbled across a notion that is now central in all his storytelling. In describing the many challenges of being a cancer patient, he said to me, "Having cancer is a full-time job." I stopped him in his tracks and told him how powerful an idea that was. Anyone who has a full-time job knows they can't have two of them. So the idea that this disease requires the kind of focus, discipline, and time as a full-time job is overwhelming. Steve started to use this phrase to set up the problem he is solving, and he said it has transformed his pitches.

Steve also read an early manuscript of this book and asked, "How can you guide innovators to make these discoveries on their own, since you won't be there to listen to their stories?" The best advice I can give is to talk with friends who aren't involved in the project and listen to hear what sticks with them. Equally importantly, just think about human nature. What is it about your story that is so human that anyone can relate to it? In Steve's case, everyone knows what it's like to have a job. That simple idea of having to manage two jobs would resonate with just about anyone. If Dottie can guide someone through their cancer care and make it less like a job, Steve's doing something important that anyone could understand.

For Komal Ahmad of Copia, she found the humanity in her story by landing on the phrase "solving the world's dumbest problem." People going hungry right down the block from an institution that is throwing out food *is* stupid. For Shilpa Shah and Karla Gallardo of the fashion brand Cuyana, it was discovering the perfect expression of their anti–fast fashion mission, "fewer, better things," which anyone with a crowded closet could relate to. For Iris Wedeking of the tooth replacement solution iDentical, it was determining exactly the best way to convey the sound of a drill to remind her audience of that awful experience in the dentist's chair. Does she bring a drill on stage and play it live? Does she use a recorded sound? Is it part of a larger video demo? What would resonate with any human at a truly visceral level?

For Surbhi Sarna, whose own life experience inspired her to create nVision Medical, it was framing her personal journey this way: "From a patient to an impatient entrepreneur." For Binta

Iliyasu, the biochemist from Niger, it was deciding to share the moment that the community elders told her to answer questions incorrectly so she wouldn't go on to become an educated woman. Every one of these human moments that the storyteller discovered made a huge difference in the impact of the stories they ultimately told.

Do Not Look into Their Eyes

I once worked with a wonderful young woman named Paulina Laurensia Ela, who works for the Borneo Orangutan Survival organization in Indonesia. When we met, she told the story of her organization and the problems it solves. She wrote a good speech, but it felt as though it was missing something. In our conversation, Paulina mentioned that she did a research project while in university at an orangutan rehabilitation center. She learned about how poachers killed young orangutans' parents so that they could steal the young babies.

Paulina mentioned that the workers at the center warned her, "When you visit the orangutan rehab center, do not look into the eyes of the young orphan orangutans. It's heartbreaking." When she arrived at the center, she couldn't help herself. She did look into their eyes, and she felt so moved that it changed her life. It's led to a career in wildlife conservation. Before we met, Paulina had not planned to share that anecdote, but once she surfaced it and included it in her story, it transformed her talk and had a huge impact on the audience. It was such a powerful and lasting image that I'm brought right back to that moment, several years ago, when Paulina shared that story with tears in her eyes.

If you're making a film, you'll ultimately have to put it in the can to meet a release date. If you're writing a book, you have to get the final version into your editor's hands before the publisher's deadline. If you're telling an innovation story, you need to finish the story before the next meeting. But unlike the other storytellers, you will have another meeting eventually. And another. Continue to polish your story until the magic emerges. Every time you tell the story, you'll have a chance to discover new techniques, language, and imagery to transform your story from good to great to "that one I'll never forget."

> ## "There is No Such Thing as Good Writing, Only Good Rewriting."

Like many great aphorisms, this quote has been attributed to many pundits, from British writer Robert Graves to Ernest Hemingway to former Supreme Court justice Louis Brandeis. Regardless, the point is that you are continually reworking your story.

Your audiences are often a great source of inspiration for rethinking or refining your story. They add value in all sorts of ways. Perhaps they'll let you know that you're not clear. Maybe they'll adore a specific part of the story. You may learn that something you said was heard in a different way than what was intended. These are all opportunities to refine or enhance the story.

I told the Mayvenn hair extensions story in class a few months ago, and a couple of Korean American students told me it had bothered them. I met with one student after class and another a bit later. They were both troubled by the way that I portrayed Korean Americans in the story. Based on their life experience, they found the story insensitive. As you'll recall, Diishan Imira set out to transform the way that Black women purchased hair and that salon owners completed the "install."

As I told the story, I mentioned that historically, Korean Americans ran the retail outlets that sold hair in the Black community. I also related that Diishan felt that some of that money for the sale of the hair to Black women should stay in the Black community. That's why he created the business and found a way to involve the stylists themselves—most of whom were Black—in the value chain. Although I had not intended for the Korean American entrepreneurs to sound like the antagonist in the story, that's the way these students had heard it. They knew how hard it was for Koreans to establish these retail businesses, starting in the 1960s. In fact, one of the students had family members in the industry. I also learned that the Rodney King protests and unrest in the 1990s further damaged relations between the Black and Korean American communities. There were wounds here. So how to evolve the story?

The fact is I'm still working on it. I could say that the retailers who traditionally sold hair in the Black communities were generally not African Americans. This way, most audience members will simply hear that there was an opportunity for the Black community to participate more in a business that serves them.

Or I could, as I chose to in this book, explain the history, acknowledge the success of the Korean entrepreneurs in building this retail industry, and be clear that Diishan did not have a problem with them. The purpose of telling the story this way is to portray the Koreans as successful innovators themselves, which they were, and hopefully, they won't come across as antagonists.

I am sure I will continue to work on this story to make sure that I'm clear, recognizing that *how* I tell it will impact whether it's making the point I want to make. As we are constantly reminded, race is complicated globally and especially in the United States. By being vulnerable and listening, we can always make our stories better. I'm grateful for the two students who came forward to share their concerns. We can all get better.

Beyond the Pitch

Story is foundational. If you can't tell someone your innovation story over lunch, in an elevator, or in a packed auditorium, then good luck moving your idea forward. But there are many other ways to get the story out into the world. Ultimately, you'll have a plethora of communication channels from which to choose, including social media, press releases, white papers, ads, sales presentations, blog posts, online videos, team meetings, investor conversations, and your digital presence. The list goes on. To strengthen your story foundation, it's useful to lock in a few elements that you can draw on regardless of the medium, including the category definition, a product descriptor, and possibly a tagline.

With these elements in place, you can engage others, especially creative specialists, to help you tell the story across all of these channels. No matter how technical a product, nailing down these components is useful. To demonstrate how this works, I'll reference the Databricks example from earlier in the book. When we created the early Databricks story, the category was Big Data as a Service; the product descriptor was a Unified Platform That Provides Easy Big Data Analysis and Processing; and the tagline was Focus on Finding Answers. With these elements and our narrative storyboard in place, we can turn this into prose.

The Databricks Story (The Narrative in Prose)

LiWei Ma is a data scientist working in a growing tech company. Given all the buzz about the power of big data, you'd think LiWei would be the most popular guy around. The executives at his company have been reading about the wonders of big data and believe that there's "gold in them thar data silos," and it's LiWei's job to find it.

But being a detective with a bunch of clunky tools isn't easy.

Some days he feels as if data science is harder than rocket science. He spends more time writing code and waiting for teams to execute it than he does looking for insights in the data. Everything is a one-off exercise.

LiWei wants to be the hero that figures out what's going on with the business, but he's spending all of his time wrestling with the tools, and the execs are growing impatient. He wishes he could just focus on finding answers in the data.

That's why the team from UC Berkeley that helped build the open-source platform Spark went on to create Databricks. They've built an integrated platform that provides easy big data analysis and processing.

First, they've created a one-stop shop for all of LiWei's data analysis and made it easy to put his data into production. Second, all of this is managed in the cloud, so there's zero management cost and it scales. And finally, LiWei enjoys the maximum speed and sophistication of the Spark stack.

Instead of tackling data headaches, LiWei can finally focus on finding answers that make an immediate impact on his business.

Databricks has already struck partnerships with Hadoop distributors, including Cloudera, IBM, MapR, and Pivotal. Hadoop is the collection of open-source utilities that facilitate using a network of computers to solve problems involving massive amounts of data and computation. This early traction in the big data ecosystem positions Databricks well to thrive in the $8.5B Unified Big Data Analytics category.

Databricks. Focus on Finding Answers.

And here's an annotated version of that same story that identifies each component of the story in **bold**.

Introduce the protagonist (the first target customer)

LiWei Ma is a data scientist working in a growing tech company. Given all the buzz about the power of big data, you'd think LiWei would be the most popular guy around. The executives at his company have been reading about the wonders of big data and believe that there's "gold in them thar data silos," and it's LiWei's job to find it.

Describe your insights about the customer's struggles (functional and emotional)

But being a detective with a bunch of clunky tools isn't easy. Some days he feels as if data science is harder than rocket science. He spends more time writing code and waiting for teams to execute it than he does looking for insights in the data. Everything is a one-off exercise. LiWei wants to be the hero that figures out what's going on with the business.

Summarize the conflict in your story; what problem are you helping your customer solve?

He's spending all of his time wrestling with the tools, and the execs are growing impatient.

Introduce the value proposition

LiWei wishes he could just *focus on finding answers* in the data.

Introduce the team

That's why the team from UC Berkeley that helped build the open-source platform Spark created Databricks.

Give a product description and provide three points to summarize how it works

They've built an *integrated platform that provides easy big data analysis and processing.* First, they've created a one-stop shop for all of LiWei's data analysis and made it easy to put his data into production. Second, all of this is managed in the cloud, so there's zero management cost and it scales. And finally, LiWei enjoys the maximum speed and sophistication of the Spark stack.

Imply how it's better than the competition

Instead of tackling data headaches, LiWei can finally focus on finding answers that make an immediate impact on his business.

Provide an example of traction and demonstrate market size

Databricks has already struck partnerships with Hadoop distributors, including Cloudera, IBM, MapR, and Pivotal. Hadoop is the collection of open-source utilities that facilitate using a network of computers to solve problems involving massive amounts of data and computation. This early traction in the big data ecosystem positions Databricks well to thrive in the $8.5B Unified Big Data Analytics category.

Reprise the vision or value proposition with a tagline

Databricks. *Focus on Finding Answers.*

When it's time to tell the story somewhere else (e.g., your website), you're ready to go. The following copy appeared on an early version of the Databricks website:

The Challenge:	Enterprises are accumulating massive quantities of data and know that there's gold inside it, and your team's job is to find it. But being a detective with a bunch of clunky tools and difficult to set up infrastructure is hard. You want to be the hero who figures out what's going on with the business, but you're spending all your time wrestling with the tools.
The Solution: Databricks Cloud	We built Databricks Cloud to make big data simple. Apache Spark made a big step towards achieving this mission by providing a unified framework for building data pipelines. Databricks Cloud takes this futher by providing a zero-management cloud platform built around Spark that delivers:

1. Fully managed Spark clusters
2. An interactive workspace for exploration and visualization
3. A production pipeline scheduler
4. A platform for powering your favorite Spark-based applications

So instead of tackling data headaches, you can finally focus on finding answers that make an immediate impact on your business.

(Copyright Databricks, 2014)

Databricks is not worth $38B today because they told a great story. They've built a fantastic business in just seven years because they *have a great story to tell*. They identified a customer in a growing category with a tremendous need, built an extraordinary technology platform to help solve their problems in a unique way, refined their business model, and executed like crazy. And yes, it didn't hurt that they spent some time at the very beginning determining what that story was and finding the simplest and most compelling way to tell it to their first employees, early customers, and founding investors. They used it to attract customers, build a great team, and raise over a billion dollars in funding.

You Have It in You

One final story. Vola Ramahery works for the Wildlife Conservation Society in Madagascar and gave a speech at an environmental leadership conference a few summers ago. I was listening to Vola rehearse the speech. She's a huge-hearted woman who wrote a lovely story about how she fell in love with the environment as a young girl. She wrote, "I lived in the city of Antananarivo in Madagascar, and it was not easy to find books to read. My school didn't have a library, and books at bookstores were expensive. I got my mom to register me at the French Cultural Center, which was one of the few places where I could access new books. On Wednesday afternoons, I walked there to borrow books. It was a three-kilometer walk from my home." She continued, "There was one magazine that I especially liked. It was called *Vintsy* after a small bird in the kingfisher family that was electric blue and brown and found only in Madagascar."[23]

---

23 Vola Ramahery, address to supporters, Beahrs Environmental Leadership Program, UC Berkeley, June 20, 2017.

"From reading *Vintsy* magazine in my young years, I fell in love with nature. I learned about nature and protected areas, and more importantly, it took me to places I would never have been able to visit. In Madagascar, most people don't have access to the country's rich wildlife as few have the means to travel around. By reading the magazine, I also became more aware of Madagascar's social and economic issues. It taught me empathy for people who are less fortunate. *Vintsy* was the first step to my future."

Vola's love affair with nature led her to eventually become an ecological innovator looking for new ways to protect Madagascar's beloved marine areas while considering the plight of local villagers who depend on the sea for their livelihoods.

It was a great story, but as Vola read it to me, something was missing. It *seemed* as if she had done everything right. She included vivid details (the vibrant colors of the kingfisher), created a sense of place (small-town Madagascar), described the challenges she overcame as a young girl (limited access to books), and explained how she ultimately conquered them to make a difference in the world (her work for the Wildlife Conservation Society). But when she read the speech, it sounded as if she had just been handed someone else's speech to read.

Story Time

I had been listening intently but asked her to stop. "Vola," I told her, "instead of reading the story, why don't you *tell* me the story." Something clicked. She looked up from her speech with a big smile on her face and said, "You mean as if I was telling a story to my two little boys?" "Yes!" I said. "Imagine that your two little boys are sitting at your feet, and you're just telling them a story. It is story time." A look of recognition spread across Vola's broad face. She *had* this! She *knew* how to tell a story. *Everyone* knows how to tell a story! She took a deep breath and went through the speech again. This time, she *told a story*. It sounded like a story. It felt like a story. I was literally speechless and a little choked up when she finished speaking. She had transported me to Madagascar with her as she shared her journey. She had completely transformed her audience's experience simply by envisioning herself sharing a tale with her two little boys back home.

Vola discovered what I hope you have discovered. Storytelling is in us. We have *evolved* to become storytellers; at some point in our life, we've all *been* storytellers. With a little effort, we can all continue to *grow* as storytellers.

> Now it's your turn.
>
> You've learned why story is essential.
>
> You've seen how to build a narrative.
>
> You've heard how to tell an emotional, clear, and compelling story.
>
> You've considered some classic story frameworks.
>
> And you know where to take your story next.
>
> Now the fun part starts. It's time to develop your great innovation story and then tell the world.
>
> It's time for you to Get Your Startup Story Straight.

Acknowledgments

They are right. It *does* take a village. The following are inhabitants of the village that supported, guided, and inspired me on the journey of writing this book.

Dana Baker-Williams, my early editor, who was invaluable in helping me to find my voice and bring form to the book.

The Greenleaf Books team, including Tiffany Barrientos, Elizabeth Brown, Corrin Foster, Neil Gonzalez, Jay Hodges, Jessica Reyes, Daniel Sandoval, and Nick Stegall, who whipped the book into shape and helped me get it out into the world.

Sara Beckman, my long-time collaborator at Berkeley-Haas School of Business, who has been a tremendous partner over the last decade as I developed my storytelling work. Sara also provided great early feedback on the book.

John Danner and Mark Coopersmith, also UC Berkeley colleagues, who provided useful insights on the process of bringing a book into the world.

Robert Grahamjones, with whom I've had conversations about storytelling on long bike rides for twenty-five years. Robert also provided great suggestions on the book's structure.

My UC Berkeley colleagues who welcomed me into their classes over the last thirteen years to develop ideas about storytelling for innovators, including Dean Rich Lyons, Dean Ann Harrison, and a host of faculty and administrators, including Adam Berman, David Charron, Bill Fanning, Jerome Engel, Mark Gorenflo, Caneel Joyce, Clark Kellogg, Vince Law, Whitney Hischier, Maura O'Neil, Mio Katayama Owens, Vivek Rao, Mike Rielly, Bill Rindfuss, David Rochlin, Frank Schultz, John Schwab, Nora Silver, Jay Stowski, and Kate Tobias.

The team at the Berkeley SkyDeck Accelerator, including Executive Director Caroline Winnett, Brian Bordley, Sibyl Chen, Bing Li, Gordon Peng, and all my early SkyDeck co-conspirators, including Clay Collier, Cathy Farmer, Tim Smith, Hilary Weber, and Alan White.

Les Schmidt (BRIIA the Intelligent Accelerator) and Marvin Liao (500 Startups), who invited me into their accelerators to do my thing (and for Marvin's advice on the book).

Stephen Bailey and Julia Alexander, cofounders of Execonline, whose platform (and partnership with Berkeley-Haas) has allowed me to teach storytelling to executives on six continents from my home office.

Eboni Freeman, Steve Derico, and Madhav Soni, innovators all and early readers of the book who provided some valuable insights.

All the extraordinary innovators, entrepreneurs, and leaders who I've met or with whom I've collaborated over the years who were the inspiration for many of the stories in the book, including Komal Ahmad, Brad Bao, Paul Birkmeyer, Ralph Clark, Matt Cooper, Thibault Duchemin, Paulina Laurensia Ela, Sasha Fisher, Andrew Gillies, Kent Frankovich, Karla Gallardo, Ali Ghodsi, Mitch Gordon, Anuj Gupta, Ben Hamlin, Ehsan Hoque, Justin Howell, Binta Iliyasu, Diishan Imira, Nick Kohut, Connor Landgraf, Dr. Panna Lossy, Shan-Lyn Ma, LiWei Ma, Samaneh Pourjalali, Pranoti Nagarkar, Vola Ramaheri, Andy Raskin, Shilpa Shah, Ion Stoica, Jonathan Tan, Maya Tobias, Iris Wedeking, Jerry Yang, and Matei Zaharia.

All my students over the past thirteen years, who taught me more than I could ever teach them.

Jon Klein, for being a lifelong friend, collaborator, and inspiration and Mike Rafael for enriching my understanding of story through our theatrical producing partnership.

My sisters, Nancy and Melissa, and my children, Jesse and Taryn, and their partners—who are all great storytellers—make me laugh and keep me humble.

My parents, Barbara and Burton Riemer, for sharing their love of stories in the form of books, movies, and theater and nurturing my storytelling jones as I grew to adulthood.

And especially my wife, Carla Riemer. Without her love and

support throughout the process (and lots of insightful feedback on the book), I would never have gotten this story straight.

About the Author

David Riemer helps entrepreneurs and innovators focus their ideas through the power of narrative. In short, he helps people get their story straight.

Earlier in his career, David was president of the ad agency J. Walter Thompson in San Francisco, held senior marketing roles at two tech startups, and was VP of Marketing at Yahoo! in its heyday.

Today, he teaches innovation methods and storytelling at Berkeley-Haas School of Business and several Bay Area accelerators. David also produces theater and serves as chair of the board of the American Conservatory Theater in San Francisco. He holds a BA from Brown University and an MBA from Columbia University.

Made in United States
North Haven, CT
19 January 2022

14981109R00121